Kindness Crusader

Kim Richardson
Publishing

Kindness Crusader

Wholesale orders can be placed by contacting the publisher, Kim Richardson.

Contact: kim.richardson@kimrichardson.kim

Compiled by: Kim Richardson
Foreword by: Emmanuel Dagher
Cover Design: Kim Richardson
Cover Photo Credit: Shutterstock – Jacob_09's

CONTENTS

FOREWORD by Emmanuel Dagher i

INTRODUCTION by Kim Richardson v

WEEK 1: NEVER UNDERESTIMATE THE POWER OF KINDNESS by Marla Goldberg 1

WEEK 2: GENTLE RAIN by Raina Irene 7

WEEK 3:CONNECTING WITH THE CURE OF KINDNESS by Talia Renzo 13

WEEK 4: MY HEART FEELS HAPPY by Sue Broome 17

WEEK 5: ROOTS OF THE GIVING TREE by Denise Manns 21

WEEK 6: ANGELS WALK AMONG US by Kelly Sunshine 25

WEEK 7: MAKING KINDNESS THE NORM by Marie Joy Monroe 31

WEEK 8: THE RIPPLE EFFECT by Georgia Nagel 37

WEEK 9: I CHOOSE KINDNESS by Heather Walker 43

WEEK 10: IT'S THE LITTLE THINGS – A KINDNESS STORY by Margaret-Maggie Honnold 47

WEEK 11: BECOMING YOUR BFF by Debora Todd 53

WEEK 12: A STURDY CONTAINER OF LIGHT by Darcie Litwicki 59

WEEK 13: LIFE LESSONS OF KINDNESS by Christine Moses 65

WEEK 14: KINDNESS IS CLEANSING by Libby Rapin 71

WEEK 15: ACCEPTING GRACE by Sheryl Goodwin-Magiera 77

WEEK 16: THROUGH TRAGEDY, KINDNESS CAN BE YOUR BIGGEST BLESSING! By Karen Hetrick 83

WEEK 17: SOUL-SISTER by Tonia Browne 89

WEEK 18: THE PATH INTO YOUR HEART by Diana Gogan 95

WEEK 19: PLANTING A SEED OF KINDNESS by Holly Bird 101

WEEK 20: FOR THE LOVE OF PUDGIE-BOO by Kris Groth 107

WEEK 21: KINDNESS 2.0 – THE NEXT GEN OF KINDNESS CRUSADERS by Nikki Griffin 113

WEEK 22: KINDNESS BEGINS WITHIN by Rochelle English 119

WEEK 23: H ELLO KINDNESS! By Krista Gawronski 123

WEEK 24: C REATE EACH DAY FROM YOUR HEART by Vicki Martinelli 129

WEEK 25: KINDNESS TURNS THE DARKNESS TO LIGHT by Grace Redman 133

WEEK 26: THE KINDNESS PROJECT by Landen Ballendine 139

WEEK 27: YES, YOU MATTER by Becca Levie 145

WEEK 28: LISTENING WITHOUT JUDGEMENT by Denise Oxley 149

WEEK 29: MAYBE by Tamara Weaver 153

WEEK 30: SPREADING KINDNESS IS AN INSIDE JOB by Paula Obeid 159

WEEK 31: DREAMS COME TRUE WHEN SUPPORTED BY KINDNESS Valerie Larson 165

WEEK 32: KINDNESS MY STRENGTH by Melanie Morrison 169

WEEK 33: KINDNESS LAID THE FOUNDATION FOR MY EXISTENCE by Toni Brucato-Kobet 173

WEEK 34: THE KINDNESS OF A STRANGER by Annemarie Lafferty 177

WEEK 35: KINDNESS AND THE POWER OF LOVING INTENTION by Erica Peace 183

WEEK 36: WANTED: SMILES & EYEBALLS by Crystal Cockerham 187

WEEK 37: THE SEED OF KINDNESS by Lana Pummill 193

WEEK 38: WWLD … WHAT WOULD LIZZIE DO? by Gina McElroy 199

WEEK 39: THE GIFT OF RECEIVING KINDNESS by Judith Manganiello 205

WEEK 40: ORDINARY, EVERYDAY ACTS OF KINDNESS by Marion Andrews 211

WEEK 41: THE GIFTS OF KINDNESS by Kelly Brickel 217

WEEK 42: A COMMUNITY OF KINDNESS by Janice Story 221

WEEK 43: KINDNESS FOR THE SOUL by Dawn Slamko 225

WEEK 44: HOW KINDNESS INSPIRED MY CHARITY by Giuliana Melo 229

WEEK 45: ACTS OF KINDNESS LEAD TO … by Lauren Raymond 233

WEEK 46: A DIVINE GIFT OF KINDNESS by Elise Schema 239

WEEK 47: YOU ARE WORTHY by Lori Geraghty 245

WEEK 48: KILL THEM WITH KINDNESS by Heather Hanson 249

WEEK 49: THE KINDLED LIFE by Antonella Lo Re 255

WEEK 50: BEING KIND TO YOURSELF RIPPLES OUT TO OTHERS by JoAnne Eisen 261

WEEK 51: KINDNESS KARMA by Carolan Dickinson 267

WEEK 52: ISLAND FAMILY OPENS THEIR HEARTS & HOME by Leann Spofford 273

CLOSING 279

CALL TO AUTHORS 281

KINDNESS CALENDARS & BINGO CARDS 283

FOREWORD

We are all born kind. It's who we inherently are at our fundamental core. If we ever witness an unkind act, we know that it is happening only because the person exhibiting this behavior learned it as a result of his or her environment or upbringing.

Being unkind stems from a need to cope or protect oneself.

With this understanding, and a bit of personal inner-healing work, we can actually grow to have compassion for those who have forgotten how to be kind to themselves and to the world around them.

Often, it's the compassion of someone else that helps bring another back to his or her authentic, kind, loving, and peaceful self.

Kindness is being able to recognize and honor the divinity in others and in ourselves without needing to place labels or judgements of any sort.

Kindness is the result of unconditional love in action.

One of the kindest people I have ever had the honor of knowing was Mrs. Wallace, my elementary school teacher.

I had just moved to the United States with my family. We came from the war-torn country of Lebanon where we had experienced great suffering, loss, and trauma.

With no understanding of the English language and having been placed in a completely different environment than I had been used to, especially at school, I began to face a brand-new set of challenges.

People looked at me as if I had landed here from a different planet. We had arrived in a small town in the Midwest where many of the locals mentioned to my family that they had never met someone from outside their state before let alone outside of the country. There were a great many unkind acts and behavior that came our way as a result, yet it felt like a piece of cake compared to what we had previously experienced in Lebanon.

One of the shining lights throughout all this integrational phase was the kindness and support of Mrs. Wallace. She helped me get through all of it.

Mrs. Wallace treated me as if I was her child. She took me under her wing and taught me how to read, write, and speak English. She spent extra time making sure I was supported. There are many teachers who do this for their students; however, Mrs. Wallace did this with a special kindness.

For the first time in my life, I felt like I was seen, heard, and honored for who I really was. Mrs. Wallace didn't want me to be anyone other than myself. She also allowed me to work at my own pace, never getting frustrated or reacting in an unkind way. Her grace, love, patience, and kindness were the greatest gifts I received from her. Looking back, I really feel as if she was an angel!

She called my parents after three months of me being in school and with joy and tears told them that it was a miracle! She said that I was beginning to understand English much faster than she had ever imagined could be possible. I look back and attest that it was because of her approach.

Children are very sensitive and intuitive beings. They feel and notice everything in their surroundings. I'm so grateful that I had a teacher who instinctively knew that and who was able to help me tremendously on my path to choosing kindness, love, and compassion.

If you ever wondered whether kindness makes a difference, please take my story into consideration. It made such a difference in my life that I have dedicated my life's work to helping others feel seen, heard, loved, and honored. It has and will always be the most rewarding gift I could ever receive.

Thank you for even reading a book like this, and for choosing to be authentically you, which is kindness in one of its many beautiful forms.

Love,

Emmanuel

EMMANUEL DAGHER serves as a teacher, author of two best-selling books, and holistic-healing facilitator, guiding tens of thousands worldwide to transform their own lives.

Emmanuel developed The Core Work Method©, a quantum healing technology that helps people recognize and resolve physical, mental, and emotional blocks that may be holding them back from living their best life.

The origins of The Core Work Method© are based on the core principles of science and spirituality—both eastern and western—and the creative and practical attributes of the right and left brain. This approach creates a whole, practical and lasting, healing experience for the recipient.

Emmanuel has shared the world stage with renowned luminaries such as Marianne Williamson, Gregg Braden, Neale Donald Walsch, Colette Baron-Reid, Carolyn Myss, Anita Moorjani, Jean Houston, and countless other distinguished thought leaders.

He has also gained widespread recognition through his philanthropic work and humanitarian efforts on behalf of refugee women and children.

Emmanuel has spoken and presented at the United Nations, the World Congress on Illumination, multiple international consulates, and countless national and international summits and events that promote peace and healing.

Connect with Emmanuel
Website: emmanueldagher.com
Facebook: emmanueldagher1
Instagram:emmanueldagherofficial

INTRODUCTION

I think we can all agree that the world could use a little more love and kindness. Can you just imagine the world if we all practiced kindness and unconditional love with each other? I like to think that one act of kindness plants the seeds for another, within us and around us. A Kindness Crusader is someone who is living the mission to plant those seeds of kindness everywhere he or she goes.

The best part of being kind is that everyone can do it! It can be anything from simple gestures like a smile and just acknowledging someone, to giving someone a helping hand or maybe helping someone who may be having a difficult time emotionally or financially. The act itself doesn't really matter; be it big or small. Sometimes the smallest acts are the ones that have the most impact.

The intention of this book is to initiate you … You are now a Kindness Crusader! Use this book as an inspirational tool so that you can plant the seeds of kindness everywhere you go. Each week there is a story to inspire you. At the back of the book, there are kindness calendars and BINGO cards. You can use the calendars and/or BINGO cards in this book, or you can download and print calendars with the dates filled, blank calendars, or blank bingo cards to create your own. Make an intention and commitment to do an act of kindness every day. Invite others to join you in your crusade of kindness. It's our job as Kindness Crusaders to continue to plant the seed of kindness every day.

I encourage you to get everyone in the home involved. Have the discussion around dinner about what acts of kindness everyone did or saw during the day. Talk about what everyone could do the next day.

You can start your own Kindness Crusader Movement in your own community. Get as many people involved as you can. Keep planting seeds and initiate new Kindness Crusaders!

Use the BINGO cards at school, work, or simply play by yourself. Have a fun reward for the winner, even if it's just you playing along.

Are you ready to make the world a better place? Join us in our Kindness Crusader Movement at KindnessCrusader.com.

Help us inspire others by sharing your stories of kindness with us on Facebook @ Kindness-Crusader and use the hashtag #kindnesscrusader when posting on Instagram or other social media platforms, we want to hear about your acts of kindness so that you will inspire others to be kind to one another!

You can download and print your Kindness Crusader calendars and Bingo game boards at KindnessCrusader.com

KIM RICHARDSON is a personal chef, mind, body, spirit practitioner, bestselling author and publisher teaching others how to live in a high vibrational place of peace, love, and joy. Through sharing her own personal experiences, she empowers individuals to transform their lives. She helps individuals to heal, forgive, and expand without judgment.

Kim teaches with unconditional love as she hopes it will have a ripple effect in the world. Her services include; health and spiritual coaching, small business consulting, book publishing, personal chef and catering, as well as transformational workshops and retreats. Be sure to visit her website to claim your free gift.

Author of the best-selling book, *High Vibe Eating, a Cookbook for your Mind, Body, and Spirit*
Publisher and co-author of the *52 Weeks of Gratitude Journal* and *Kindness Crusader*
Coauthor of *Living Your Purpose*, *365 Days of Angel Prayers*, and *Spiritual Leaders Top Picks*

Connect with Kim
Website: KimRichardson.Kim
Facebook: kimrichardson444
Email: Kim.Richardson@KimRichardson.Kim

Week 1

Sometimes it takes only one act of kindness and caring to change a person's life.

~ Jackie Chan

NEVER UNDERESTIMATE THE POWER OF KINDNESS

In today's current climate of increasing anger, hate, and bigotry, I work hard to offset those same energies in my life. I do that by making a concerted effort to be kind to every being I meet by sharing a nice word or a compliment, with random acts, and by supporting those who come to me who share intimate details of their lives.

So many people walk around spewing negative thoughts, words, and deeds without an understanding of the negative energetic impact that will not only come back to them tenfold but will trickle out and affect many unsuspecting individuals in the process. This is a piece of the Law of Attraction.

What is the Law of Attraction? According to The Law of Attraction's website, it's "the ability to attract into our lives whatever we are focusing on."

The website continues, "All thoughts turn into things eventually. If you focus on doom and gloom, you will remain under that cloud. If you focus on positive thoughts and have goals that you aim to achieve, you will find a way to achieve them with massive action."

Kindness is under the umbrella of positivity. Kindness has the power to change the energy of each of our lives, which in turn has a multiplicative affect – changing the lives of millions of people.

Have you ever noticed that when you offer a kind gesture to someone how much better it makes you feel? Acts of kindness are varied in nature. It could be rescuing a stray dog or an injured animal. It might be listening to someone who just needs an empathic ear to hear his or her story.

Offering a gesture of kindness makes my heart skip a beat with joy. It brings me pleasure and gratification to know that a kind word or gesture made a positive difference in someone else's life.

I've read stories of people who have performed heroic acts, such as the boys who came across a dog stuck in rushing water. The circumstances were dire and instead of letting the dog be swept away or drown, these boys turned into a human chain to get the dog to safety, risking their own lives in the process.

There's the story of a sloth stuck on rocks unable to get to a tree. A man saw this sloth that appeared to be exhausted and tired. The gentleman found a branch and he was able to coax the sloth onto the branch then walk over difficult rocky terrain, found a good, strong tree and gave the sloth a safe place to regain his strength.

How about the driver of a car who sees an old person struggling to cross a busy street and pulls over, stopping traffic to help that individual safely across?

Do you wonder how these people feel after they helped the stuck dog, exhausted sloth, or senior? I can't say for sure, but intuitively I feel that they may have felt happy and proud and perhaps had even a sense of accomplishment that they were able to help someone or something in need.

I've never been called upon to help someone in a dangerous situation, but I make a concerted effort each day to be kind to one and all.

I was recently in Bali. As is in the case in too many other countries, Bali has an abundance of stray dogs in need of care. They are amazing to me. Though under- nourished and untrained and not cared for, these animals are resilient and demonstrate their ability to keep moving forward. They will even look both ways when they cross the street.

Those who know me understand that I have a soft spot for animals, especially dogs and horses. During my visit to Bali, I would go to the local store and purchase dog treats to keep in my purse. When I came upon dogs that looked like they needed sustenance, I would offer them a few cookies. It may not have been a full meal, but I hope it helped to curb any hunger they had, and they knew that someone felt something for them.

As a professional healer, my desire is always to help others. As an intuitive and an empath, I can observe and feel someone else's energy and get an idea of what is going on with them. From my life experiences, I know that a kind word or gesture can make a difference in a person's day, or possibly her or his outlook on a part of life.

I was recently having a conversation with a young girl who had been experiencing bouts of depression and anxiety. She shared with me how the doctor had prescribed medication to her that made her feel like a zombie and how she hated feeling that way. After some time of taking the medication, this girl made a decision to change the way she handled her anxiety and depression. She was successfully able to wean herself off the medication and take control of her life. She went on to share how she went back to school and how much her recent graduation meant to her. She continued to share with me how well she's functioning and how good she feels.

When I congratulated her on her successes and pointed out how much strength and fortitude it took for her to get off her meds and to take control of her life, she looked at me with this an odd expression on her face. Then her face took on a wonderful glow of pride and joy. She didn't realize how much courage and strength it took to change her circumstances and what a powerful change that made in her life. She was lit up like a Christmas tree. It's funny how a few kind words can help someone to see him or herself with a fresh and positive perspective.

I'd like to end with a reminder to never underestimate the power of kindness whether in word or deed. It can make a positive difference, not only in someone's life, but also in your own.

MARLA GOLDBERG is an energy healer, intuitive, speaker, host of the "Guided Spirit Conversations" podcast on Voice America, and bestselling author of *My F*cking Long Journey to Loving Myself: A Guide to a Shorter Path.*

Marla began her spiritual journey when her life hit rock bottom. Serendipitously around the same time, she met her first spiritual teacher and attended her first mystery school. After graduation, Marla continued learning new techniques and today has been trained in twenty-four different techniques.

Marla works with clients all over the world to help them shift or enhance their lives through intuitive guidance and her various methods.

Connect with Marla
Website: marlagoldberg.net
Email: marla@mghealer.com
Phone: 847-275-5584

Week 2

Do things for people not because of who they are or what they do in return, but because of who you are.

~ Harold S. Kushner

GENTLE RAIN

Unfathomable with the hidden parts of my soul I cry, the gentle rain from my broken heart beckons for absolution. From exhaustion, I beg for slumber that shuns me.

This mantra replaced the hymn I once sang. My beautiful twenty-nine-year-old son had been stolen from me; the earth and its forest had swallowed him on a warm October Sunday in 2017. Josiah, my youngest child, thought today was as perfect as any other day. So perfect, he thought a motorcycle ride deep into the forest of Santa Cruz would only enhance the journey of his day. He straddled the bike, owning the road he would travel. Deep within the forest, I believe the tree elves beckoned him. As they caught his attention, he realized they were showing him a portal; a doorway to the spirit realm. Josiah loved the earth elements, the sky angels, and anything that spoke of higher dimensions. So, it is without question he wanted to go the way they beckoned. Leaving his body and the motorcycle unattended, it met the tree that sealed the portal.

Is this the fairy tale I tell myself or is this the truth of the elements, the angels, spirit, and the universe that compels us? His entrance to spirit; my entrance to unimaginable sorrow. A pain with an identity that demanded attention. Left to its own will, it would have consumed me and led me directly to that same portal.

Who am I now? I am no longer me, I'm grief; doubling as wife, mother, grandmother, sister, and friend. When someone so close to you leaves this planet, it stops you, stunts you. The unanswered questions haunt you. You turn inward towards guilt and despair. The *I should have and why didn't I?* play on a loop. Everything about you is in question.

I had to find the answers.

What does this have to do with kindness? Everything.

We have all experienced the profound despair that leaves us broken. Taking responsibility for other people's stories, deeming it our fault, and creating such unkindness within ourselves.

"If only I would have called him that morning, he would have told me he was going on that ride and I could have pressured him into not going."

"If only I would have forced him to do this differently or that."

"If only I would have loved him more."

"Why didn't I call, oh G~d, why didn't I call him?"

Tears pouring inward as well as outward, each one producing more guilt and responsibility than the next.

"Josiah I am so sorry," I lamented, walking across the family room of my home. Speaking out loud how guilty I felt. I picked up a deck of cards titled, "Talking to Heaven." As I shuffled them, a card fell to the floor facing upwards so I could see it. I inhaled and held my breath as if I would never breathe again. Yet he was pressing me to breathe and continue, the card read, "It is not your fault."

I fell to my knees, uncontrollably weeping as I pressed the card against my chest, begging this truth to enter my heart.

"Josiah!" I bellowed. "How is this possible?"

I laid on the floor until the pouring turned to the gentle rain of calm. When I finally stood up, I felt hungry. I glanced around the room bewildered. Had I eaten today? And if I had, was it something other than peanut butter, pita chips, or coffee? My grief so prominent, it excluded all else, including taking care of myself. I had stopped being kind to myself. How can kindness matter if I didn't?

Josiah is not here with me in the physical and that is unnervingly heart-wrenching; that will never go away, in truth I never want it to. I never want to not feel the magnitude of who he is and what he represents to me and my family, and the impact he had and continues to have on all of us. Let the tears flow, the continuous gentle rain of love, not guilt and responsibility. Sorrow mixed with the jewel of Josiah, his sibling, my grandchildren and all the love that surrounds me, I walked into the kitchen. Staring into the refrigerator; I am still not hungry. Laughter was going to take some time to return. It would take over a year before I could truly exercise again and be physically present in my body. I wasn't going to feel right for a while, but I was going to stop telling myself I did something wrong.

We had a destiny. I signed a contract with him. This time he was my son. Last time, I am pretty sure he was my father, but none of that matters. What matters is that he and I continue. Not as we were, but as we are now. Without kindness to myself and giving myself grace in the line of fire, I would not have been able to continue. I had to give myself some sympathy and understanding for the new me.

Dark despair, trauma, and even drama create the next version of our tapestry, weaving through our hearts with golden threads, filling in the broken lines. I understand, I had to feel every one of those tortured emotions. There is no escaping them. Everything we go through defines us. Life dictates and we must take notes. Pondering the pain is necessary; the beatings we give ourselves are far worse than what others could give us. Life can be so cruel; we must not be cruel to ourselves.

My relationship with Josiah in spirit is strong, mixed with tears, agony, amazement and gratitude. I would not be able to see this if I stayed in shame and blame. Does it rear its disgustingly ugly head at me? Yes. I'm not going to lie to you. I'm a mother devastated by the unimaginable. Yet out of what we cannot imagine, we press on to imagine something bondless. The ability to survive through sorrow and find our way back to the ones we thought were out of reach.

Love has no limit and death is an illusion, a symphony of painful chords; and if we can see this pain as our own portal. A doorway to our higher dimension. That those same tree elves and sky angels that beckoned my son, also beckon me to a place where unconditional love abounds. Wouldn't that include unconditional love for myself? Why yes, it would.

I forced myself to eat. I had forgotten how good food tasted. I had forgotten the clarity that comes from nourishing myself. I looked outside the window. The sun was shining, even the outdoors seemed foreign. I took my journal outside, and invited vitamin D from the sun's rays onto my skin. The thunderstorm of my soul began to still. My pen began to dance across the blue that lined the pages, creating words that were not mine.

"Breathe, just breathe, Raina. There has been too much going on in your head. You have logged everything, and it is wearing you thin. Be, just be. There are still moments to be had that Josiah will be with you in. I promise; it is not over. He is here and will be with you in all things you do, outside with your animals and inside your spirit. Breathe. Take in the newness of his energy. He is asking you to pause and feel him, pause and see him, pause and hear him. Dry your tears, Raina. He is here. Close your eyes, Raina. He is here. See him. Open your heart, Raina. Open it. Write. Let it in. Let in this new energy. Let this vibration in. It is Josiah."

I looked down at the page before me. Who had written this? It wasn't from Josiah or it would have read 'Mom.' Was it me channeling me? Was it the earth elements or the sky angels? It didn't really matter. The message was clear: my Son is here. He is with me and that wasn't going to change. What had to change was me. I had to give up the story where I held it was my fault and give it back to the universe.

I create another letter. It had all my misconstrued interpretations of my part, however it poured out of me, I let the floodgates open. Once I felt a shift, I knew I was done. I lit the fire pit that would dissipate the evidence of these false feelings. It's amazing how the universe responds. As I sat outside witnessing these emotions burning to ashes and wondering if I might have left a few notes inside myself for further beatings, a gentle rain began to sprinkle amid the embers. The tears of my heart collapsed the entire sky above me, gently cleansing me, and reminding me once more, that I had been heard.

RAINA IRENE is a Heart, Soul, Spirit Practitioner and the owner of Beauty, Strength & Healing Inc. She holds multiple certificates in Holistic Health, Spiritual Work, Emotional Healing and is a licensed Esthetician.

Raina's Eclectic and Spiritual diversity enables her to tap into your unique needs, supporting and guiding you to clarity and connecting you with your own healing energies. She blends her esthetics with intuition; councils one on one; holds healing circles with the emphasis on inner wisdom and understanding grief.

With two Siblings, Parents and now Son in Spirit, Raina has devoted herself to sharing that our bonds continue, and Love is forever … all you have to do is *believe* and you will see.

Connect with Raina

Facebook: GypsyRaina.Irene
Facebook: gypsyraina
Join her Facebook group at: BeautyStrengthHealing

If you have a child in Spirit or would like to share with a friend who does, join her Facebook group: facebook.com/groups/lullabyletters

Week 3

Carry out a random act of kindness, with no expectation of reward, safe in the knowledge that one day someone might do the same for you.

~ Princess Diana

CONNECTING WITH THE CURE OF KINDNESS

How often do you feel like you have lost control? Like you have lost your power? Now, how often do you redirect those feelings into positivity? When we redirect negative energy into a vortex of kindness, inwards or outwards, we are transforming not just the current perception of our own lives, but even the life of somebody else.

Kindness is an achievable practice. It's one of the few practices in life that requires little to no money. When it is achieved at its minimum, we are expanding its meaning to the maximum. Kindness does not require a reason. When we adopt kindness into our daily life and routine, we are creating a space in our hearts that gives so much love and receiving so much more in return.

Kindness can heal. If you need healing in your life, it's best not to look outward for help, validation, or void fillers. To truly feel a difference in your day of healing, practice one random act of kindness at a time. A random act of kindness is a selfless and random act performed for another individual that brings them joy at that moment. Random acts of kindness range from a simple compliment to another person in a grocery store, purchasing somebody's drink in the Starbucks drive-through, helping a family member by running a chore or an errand, helping an elderly individual across the street, to helping your neighbor with landscaping. All of these random acts of kindness come at an opportune time by your choice. By performing these selfless acts, you are not only strengthening the trust and hearts of those around you, but you are healing your heart in the process.

It may come as a surprise when I tell you that kindness is always a two-way street. Even when we are the only ones performing the act, we are receiving so much in return that we don't realize at that moment. Reflect on the last time you performed a random act of kindness and remember how good it made you feel. I can promise you one thing, you can never walk away after performing an act of kindness, angry or sad. Kindness holds so much power to not only change your day but brings you closer to a satisfying state of peace and happiness.

Kindness brings us all the company that we need. In moments of our loneliness, and isolation, we must befriend kindness.

We talked about the result of directing kindness outwards, but what happens when we direct kindness inwards? When we internalize kindness, we are self-healing. The days that we feel the most discouraged are the days we must be the kindest to ourselves. Rather than expressing your frustration with hate, additional pain, or further complications, you can change your thoughts. Change your outlook on how you talk to and about yourself.

When you look in the mirror and say, "I am a failure," you become one. Instead, look in the mirror and say, "Today was a difficult day, but I am not going to cry about it and feel bad for myself." Be the kindest you can be to yourself at that moment and redirect your energy and attitude.

When we experience waves of depression, sadness, and anxiety is when self-love and self-care must become a priority. When we are amid a discouraging heartbreak, breakup, or loss, that's when kindness is the most necessary. Maintaining good mental and physical health is a form of self-kindness. Taking yourself on a walk, going out to lunch, seeing a movie, bathing yourself, cooking for yourself, cleaning up after yourself, and getting a pedicure are all self-caring ways of being kind. When we do these things regularly, we are not only taking care of ourselves, we are internalizing the practices of kindness.

Kindness fills the emptiness in our lives. Even on the worst of our days, if we practice giving or receiving kindness, we are becoming the best versions of ourselves that we can be.

I've learned from my personal experiences as a barista at Starbucks that kindness is so necessary. My goal was to be kind to everybody, especially to those who needed it the most. I learned the hard way that when people were rude, impatient, or unkind, I had to be the complete opposite of what they were in that moment and take on the responsibility of delivering the kindness that they had been missing in their days. As emotionally exhausting as it was, it strengthened me to lift myself as well as others. If you are constantly in an atmosphere where you are surrounded by negativity at your job or in a particularly negative relationship, chances are, you will feel drained. When these atmospheres exhaust your energy, replenish the roots of your ground by spreading kindness. Always remember that kindness always never drains. Fill yourself with the right intention and watch your spirit blossom where it is planted. Kindness is a daily practice. You can make the world a kinder place. Share this power with those around you, and especially with those that need it the most in their day.

TALIA RENZO was bullied in school at a young age and her dad passed away unexpectedly. Talia was abandoned not long after her dad died. As she experienced great loss, it brought her to a higher appreciation for wisdom. Talia decided not to fall the same way as everyone else did through life's greatest trials. Instead, she took all her pain and channeled it into passionate writing and pearls of wisdom.

She wrote her first book at sixteen years old and has taken to writing for her own healing and to share inspiration for others in need of love, healing, and wisdom. Visit her website for more poetry, updates, and wisdom.

Connect with Talia
Website: taliarenzo.com
Facebook: taliarenzo

Week 4

Because that's what kindness is. It's not doing something for someone else because they can't, but because you can.

~ Andrew Iskander

MY HEART FEELS HAPPY

I believe acts of kindness are underestimated. Many do not realize the immense impact a simple act of being kind can have on themselves, other people, animals, Mother Earth and the environment.

One of the pictures the angels have shared with me is one person taking and holding the hand of another and that person taking and holding the hand of the next and so on and so on. The first person taking the hand of another is an act of kindness. Maybe they are helping someone from a fall or maybe they are helping someone off the side of a bridge. Each person adding their helping hand strengthens the initial act of kindness. It expands energetically and moves to a higher vibration. Think of a pebble in a pond, the ripples getting larger and ever expanding.

We can each be a part of this kindness chain. We do not need to stand alone. When we reach out with kindness to another, it opens doors of possibilities for ourselves as well as for others. It also has a way of clearing our minds of clutter that may be stored within. When we feel unsure of the next step to take, being kind to another takes our focus from ourselves and what is happening in our lives. It allows ideas and solutions to be presented.

The intention in doing an act of kindness is key. The perfect recipe is when it's coming from a pure heart, filled with love, and with no expectation of anything in return. The angels stand with us for each act of kindness. They are adding their love to the mix as well.

A side effect of being kind is you may find yourself feeling happier for no apparent reason. You may notice the flow of your day seems to be much smoother and even if something rocks the boat a bit, it will be slight rather than bouncing back and forth. You will also come back to center much more quickly and easily.

Let me share a short story: Once upon a time there was a little girl. She did not have a lot of friends though she had her pets and she had the trees and the animals in the forest. She would find herself having her own version of a tea party with her kitty and her puppy while the bunnies and the squirrels watched at a safe distance.

She would pour the "tea" for her pets always before she would pour for herself. She would serve the tasty treats to everyone else before she would take even the tiniest of tastes. She didn't do this because she thought about being kind. She did it because her heart felt better when she did. It felt as though it was being gently massaged with love every time she was kind to another. It seemed to automatically spill into her home life. She'd help out with the chores where she could and offered a smile or a funny story when it was a task she couldn't do.

As she grew into adulthood, she continued being kind to everyone she met, whether acknowledged or not. Her heart felt happy. As an adult, she continued being kind to all she met.

Along the way, she realized that being kind to herself was an important piece. For her, being kind to others felt as though she was also being kind to herself. And her heart always felt happy.

See if your heart feels happy with this challenge I have for you. Smile at every person you see. I am talking about the person in the mirror, the person you glance at in the car next to you at the stoplight, the grocery store clerk as you catch his or her eye, or the person next to you in line. Every person you see today, smile. Smile with your eyes as well as your lips. Feel the kindness expand from within so that it encompasses your whole being and feel the happiness in your heart expand. You may also feel the angels smiling with you as they offer their love.

Angel Blessings to you,

Sue

SUE BROOME is a gifted intuitive healer, spiritual teacher, and author. She works with the divine and angels in guiding others on their spiritual healing journey. Through her products, workshops, and healing sessions, she guides others with tools of empowerment. She believes that you having the tools you need for your spiritual healing journey is key.

To learn more about Sue and to receive a free PDF, *Healing Tools From the Angels*, go to: Empowerment4You.com/angel-talk-with-sue.

Connect with Sue
Email: su.broome@gmail.com
Website: Empowerment4You.com
Facebook: Empowerment4You
Instagram: @SueBroome44
YouTube Channel: SueBroome

Week 5

Love and kindness are never wasted. They always make a difference. They bless the one who receives them, and they bless you, the giver.

~ Barbara De Angelis

ROOTS OF THE GIVING TREE

Dear Mom,

This is a very belated thank you for your lessons in kindness.

You were wholeheartedly accepting of me no matter what. Well okay, except for that time when I was mouthing off in the car, and you made me get out and walk two miles home. I have no recollection what I actually did or said. It's a funny thing how selective a teenage memory can be. I know that it had to be pretty bad because you had what seemed like an endless rope of patience, and the rope snapped that day. I was unkind and clearly disrespectful, or you would have not dropped my sad-sack self, off in a parking lot to walk home alone in the dark.

I remember crying on my way home, feeling like I was a victim. I remember being angry that you made me walk. In retrospect, the long walk allowed me the time to reflect and realize that I messed up. I remember the gut-wrenching feeling of regret. It must have taken a lot for you to have to draw such a boundary with me. I was always the rule-follower. I was not a problem child. Ha! It may not have been a journey of a thousand miles, even though it felt like it, but it sure was a journey of growth.

That single event ingrained my deep humility. I learned the power of my words and actions and how they affect others. I learned how important it is to be gentle, especially to those closest to me, those that I might take for granted.

BRAVO, MOM!

Thanks to my mother, I received the best lesson I ever learned in my teenage years, *and* one of the best I ever learned in my entire life. It was so impactful that I am writing about it forty years later.

BE KIND.

I know that in the future, inevitably if (when) I mess up again, then I can be humble enough to accept it, admit it, and apologize. Forgiveness is such a beautiful and mutual gift.

There you were, an unconditionally loving, deeply devoted mother in the midst of your own healing crisis at the age of forty. What did I know at sixteen? Not much for sure!

Thank goodness for your years of modeling extreme patience and unconditional compassion. You saw the good in others and beamed it out like a beacon light. Your goodwill in daily life and in your teachings at our county prison most certainly modeled exemplary behavior to emulate. You believed there was good in the world. You didn't have to preach kindness; you demonstrated it with grace and ease.

In your life, you represented the book, *The Giving Tree*, and you were that tree in my world. I like to think I have the roots of your giving tree deep within, grounding me. I hold strongly to your gift of giving to others, your unfailing caring, and your humble kindness. You showed me I don't have to be a martyr to be kind. I am attached to humanity through a reciprocal rope of giving and receiving. And while that rope can have kinks, or even be frayed in places, it can be repaired and strengthened.

It's been twenty-five years since you moved on from this earthly realm. Yeah, I know this letter is way overdue, but I am eternally grateful for the time I had under your kindness tutelage. I embrace the essence of kindness through respect, compassion, and caring. I choose to believe there is good in the world. I choose to be the change instead of being a bystander. I hope I am stepping up to the plate enough with my conscious words and actions. I hope I am modeling the goodness that you showed me exists in the world. I bear the proud banner of a kindness crusader in my heart, in my mind, and in my soul.

Kindness flows within me and around me. I share it with the world.

DENISE MANNS is a perpetually passionate student, an enthusiastic educator, and a humanitarian at heart with careers in public education, counseling, and manual therapies.

Her mission is to promote wellness, spread joy, and ignite compassionate individual empowerment. Her ultimate dream is to see each and every human find his or her own personal, soul-fulfilling *Happy*.

She is founder and facilitator of HappyHuman, LLC, a company devoted to optimal mental, physical, emotional, and spiritual wellness.

Her home base is Traverse City, Michigan.

Connect with Denise
Website: happyhumannow.com
Email: happyhumannow@gmail.com

Week 6

We can't help everyone, but everyone can help someone.

~ Ronald Reagan

ANGELS WALK AMONG US

As I sat there in the waiting room with my husband, Brad, that Wednesday afternoon, I tried to stuff my feelings of hopelessness and think positively. But when I looked down at my hands folded in my lap, a sudden wave of dread washed over me; I had forgotten to wear my angels!

"Of all the days," I thought to myself. "This is when I needed their comfort the most!"

I had been depending on my silver, angel, charm bracelet from my mom since the Saturday before. It was meant to help me through the most difficult week of my life.

Brad had been sick for the past two months with what our family physician diagnosed as acute bronchitis. But he was only getting worse, so the Friday before our hospital visit I had asked him to go back to the doctor to explain in detail exactly how bad it was and ask for a chest x-ray.

I said, "Tell him you've lost twenty pounds in the past two weeks and that you don't even want beer or chocolate, which means something is very wrong. Explain that you can't talk for more than a couple of minutes before going into an uncontrollable coughing fit. Tell him that we change the bed sheets twice each night because you sweat so profusely." He asked me to write it all down, and then he handed my note to the doctor. He got the x-ray, and later that night we got the news that it showed probable lymphoma.

As soon as we heard those words, we called my parents who are both nurses and his uncle who was a doctor. All three told us to get to the Stanford emergency room that weekend, so we did. After the chief physician examined Brad, he said he wanted to speed up the process by ordering a biopsy of the enlarged lymph node he'd found in Brad's neck. That was how we found ourselves silently side-by-side in the well-worn hospital chairs.

Part of the reason for my silence was what I was trying hard *not* to tell Brad: that when I got to work that morning, I found out I was going to lose my job the next day. I was part of the massive layoff my company regretfully announced.

Finally, the nurse took us back to the exam room, and I grabbed Brad's hand, staring at my wrist where my angels should be dangling. They performed the biopsy, looked at his x-ray, then disclosed that based on his advanced symptoms, they were certain he had cancer. The next step was an immediate appointment with an oncologist to determine the exact diagnosis and explain his treatment options.

I remember it felt like we were moving in slow motion as walked out of the building. Once we got to the car, Brad just crawled into the backseat and fell asleep. My thoughts bounced from what the Stanford experts had just revealed to everything that had transpired at work since I had told my manager why I needed this afternoon off. Her mother had recently died of breast cancer, so she was extremely supportive. As I prepared to leave for Brad's appointment, Robert, the director of our department, stopped by my desk. He told me that he'd heard what I was going through and expressed how sorry he was. He said that family comes first and then asked me to try *not* to worry about what was happening in the office in order to focus on what was most important.

We got home around 6:00 p.m., and I started making dinner. I couldn't stop thinking about the gravity of our situation. My husband had a life-threatening illness; he could lose his commission-only sales job depending on how rigorous the treatment was, and I was definitely losing mine. At a time when he needed all his strength to try and fight this disease, the financial stress could be devastating. I didn't know what to do.

I ran through a few scenarios in my head. I could just tell him my news; we could get all the bad crap out on the table, then tomorrow figure out how we're going to tackle it together. I could say nothing and finish out the week pretending to go to work each day as I figured out how to get a new job while five months pregnant and caring for a cancer patient. Or, I could say nothing that night, then come home from work early the next day with my pink slip in hand.

I just couldn't stomach the second or third choices. I'd never kept secrets from him and couldn't imagine being able to fake going to work, pretending that all was okay. If I waited until the next day, he might decide the bad news was never-ending and be left feeling utterly defeated.

So as he laid down to rest, I said, "I have something to tell you."

When I was done, he looked at me in disbelief at our reality, then he completely passed out on the couch. At this point, I started questioning God. Why us? We'd been happily married for just a little more than a year, were blessed with jobs we loved, had just bought a house to make our own, and were expecting our first child.

At 11:01 p.m. the phone rang, and I wondered who in the heck was calling that late. It was my human-resources manager calling to talk about my job. I told her I knew what to expect.

"That's just it," she said. "I have something important to tell you. I debated calling but figured it might help you to know the whole story."

I was thoroughly confused.

She continued, "Robert told me about your situation, and I'm so sorry. This afternoon he came charging into my office as we were drafting the list of employees for the layoff, and insisted that we find a way to keep you on, at least until your maternity leave. He was so adamant, he said if we couldn't justify paying your salary, we were to take the money for *you* out of *his*."

I couldn't believe what I was hearing.

"Kelly, you get to keep your job!"

She went on to explain that they had to do some restructuring of the company due to the diminished workforce. They decided since I was one of the first hired and my manager needed assistance to keep things afloat, it made sense to retain my position. She reassured me that they were able to pay me without taking anything away from my boss. And although he didn't want me to know what he'd proposed, she was going against his wishes because she felt that knowing might give me comfort and hope when I need it most.

I thanked her and as I hung up the phone, I felt a profound sense of relief and gratitude. I realized that when we were in the waiting room and I noticed I'd forgotten my angels; my angels hadn't forgotten me. In fact, at that very moment, there was a human in my life who became my angel.

KELLY SUNSHINE enjoys living in beautiful Petaluma, CA. She began her career as an ESL/EFL teacher at the college level and delighted in learning about other people and cultures. At a time when full-time teaching got harder to find, she branched off into other roles, such as becoming a caseworker and corporate trainer.

While spending several years as a stay-at-home mom of two, she never lost her passion as a wordsmith, which she turned into a business. Now, she is a dedicated copywriter and editor, with her own young-adult fiction novel in the works.

Connect with Kelly
Website: kellysunshine.journoportfolio.com
Email: kellysunshinestoryteller@gmail.com
Facebook: getitdonewrite
Facebook: growglobalgoodness
Instagram: growglobalgoodness
Instagram: kelly_sunshine5
Cell: 650-533-3181

Week 7

Unexpected kindness is the most powerful, least costly, and most underrated agent of human change.

~ Bob Kerrey

MAKING KINDNESS THE NORM

PERFORMING DELIBERATE ACTS OF
KINDNESS RATHER THAN RANDOM ONES

Kindness. It's a word that's frequently iterated, but what does it really mean? The *Oxford English Dictionary* defines kindness as "the quality of being friendly, generous, and considerate; a kind act." Kindness can be as simple as genuinely smiling at someone who looks sad or something a bit nobler such as buying groceries for a family in need. Looking up from your phone and making eye contact with someone, giving a hug or a simple squeeze of someone's hand when they are downhearted can make a meaningful and long-lasting impact.

Recently, I sent out an informal survey to many friends and associates. The survey participants included people from many walks of life from all over the country. While they were all vastly different individuals, their responses were remarkably similar. The survey consisted of three simple questions:

1. What does kindness mean to you?

2. How has kindness impacted your life?

3. Do you believe that kindness could change the world?

Most participants defined kindness in a manner comparable to the dictionary's definition of being friendly, generous, and considerate. Some delved a bit deeper and mentioned respect, empathy, connection, tolerance, and forgiveness. A common theme was how kindness was evidenced by action. Doing something for someone else without expectation of receiving anything in return was frequently expressed. One friend said that kindness had strongly impacted him into becoming a better person of faith. Another said that kindness impacted him the most when it was shown to him even though he deserved the opposite at that moment. Everyone used different verbiage to describe kindness, yet the remarkable similarity was everyone's answer to the third question, which was unanimously positive. Every response to being asked if they believed kindness could change the world was a resounding, "*YES!*" This affirmed my belief that kindness can indeed change the world.

The movie, *Pay it Forward* has had a profound effect on me. While it requires a box of tissues to get through, I've watched it many times. The character of Trevor McKinney, played by Haley Joel Osment, is a twelve-year-old boy who is given an assignment of creating a plan for changing the world. He devised a plan to pay it forward. One would perform a kind act for someone. The only way that the recipient of your kindness had to pay you back was to do something kind for three different people, thus paying it forward. The three recipients would then repeat the cycle. Trevor drew a tree-like diagram on a blackboard with branches extending for each kind act. If we all adapted this kindness crusade and sowed the seeds of kindness, then change would be eminent. Imagine how large the kindness tree would grow! The effects of one act of kindness would be exponential.

Kindness not only benefits the recipient. In an article, *The Importance of Kindness* in *Psychology Today*, Dr. Karyn Hall stated that, "Science has now shown that devoting resources to others, rather than having more and more for yourself, brings about lasting well-being." By being kind or giving to others in need, you benefit as well. Kindness often has an equal or greater effect on the giver. In *The Five Side Effects of Kindness*, Dr. David R. Hamilton asserts that, "Kindness makes us happier, is good for the heart, slows ageing, improves relationships and is contagious." Studies have even shown that simply witnessing an act of kindness can have beneficial health and emotional effects.

Sometimes kindness involves the simple act of inclusion. Inviting that annoying, negative, less-than-favorite coworker to lunch doesn't necessarily sound like fun. However, you could make a great difference in that person's life. Who knows, you might even make a new friend. Spending just a little time with her might put a smile on her face and touch her heart. Inclusion might not change the entire world, but it could change one person's world.

Bullying, especially with regard to children, seems to be much more prevalent than in the past. While I won't even pretend to be an expert on human behavior, I would contend that kindness is innate in humans. It is human nature to want to help. Unkindness is usually a learned behavior. Children emulate what they see and hear. So much negativity is being expressed daily in the media, oftentimes by so-called leaders that it's no wonder some children bully others. Frequently, bullies are lonely, acting out, and emulating the behavior that they see in the media and – God forbid – at home.

Kindness begins at home. Not tolerating bullying and unkindness as well as invoking a spirit of deliberate kindness are examples for the next generation. What if we encouraged our children and grandchildren to be inclusive of that weird or lonely child? What if we turned the television off when something negative was on and watched something positive together or played a game as a family? What if we talked with our children about something negative, they'd heard and emphasize how that's not acceptable behavior even if the negative behavior was being demonstrated by someone in a position of authority?

Kindness has had a profound effect on my life. Conversely, unkindness has also impacted me. We can all recollect both kindness and unkindness from years ago. One act of kindness bestowed upon me was shortly after my first child was born and finances were really tight. A friend gave me seven huge bags stuffed with infant and toddler clothing. A friend of hers had given them to her and asked her to give them to me. It made me cry and I vividly remember it now, decades later. The kindness of a woman who I have still have never met made a profound impact upon my heart. Over the years, I have helped out several young mothers because of what this woman did for me. The memory of a woman's generosity and kindness inspired me to pay it forward.

We remember kind acts for a lifetime, but unfortunately sometimes we choose to focus on unkind acts and how bad they make us feel. Using those unkind experiences as a learning tool of what not to do to others is much more advantageous to self-care than dwelling upon them.

There's been a lot of talk about random acts of kindness. It has become a somewhat clichéd phrase and even put on bumper stickers. Books have been written about it. While the act of buying a cup of coffee for next person in line, holding a door for a stranger, saying hello, and genuinely smiling at someone we encounter is kind, shouldn't that be the norm rather than the exception? What if we began performing *deliberate* acts of kindness rather than simply random ones? What if every day we deliberately purposed to be kind even when it was difficult? Kindness begins with you and me. Kindness makes a difference in the lives of others as well as our own. It's even good for our health! It might seem far-fetched, but together we can change the world, one deliberate act of kindness at a time.

In the words of John Lennon, *"Imagine all the people, living life in peace. You may say that I'm a dreamer ... but I'm not the only one."*

Surely, I am not the only one. Starting today, I challenge you to be deliberately kind even when it's difficult. I will personally take on this challenge as well. Let's start performing deliberate acts of kindness and make kindness the norm.

MARIE JOY MONROE is the author of the award-winning children's book, *Buddy the Soldier Bear,* which gives back to nonprofits who serve our veterans. She is an Air Force "brat" and Army mom. Marie hopes to inspire children to dream big, be kind, and give back.

She has worked as a success coach for military online college students. She's a member of the Blue Star Moms of the Southwest Valley. In her spare time, she volunteers, sends care packages to deployed soldiers, and is working on several writing projects. Marie is delighted to be a part of the Kindness Crusade!

Connect with Marie Joy
Website: mariejoywrites.com
Website: buddythesoldierbear.com
Facebook: mariejoywrites
Instagram mariejoywrites
Twitter mariejoywrites

Week 8

Constant kindness can accomplish much. As the sun makes ice melt, kindness causes misunderstanding, mistrust, and hostility to evaporate.

~ Albert Schweitzer

THE RIPPLE EFFECT

For over two months at noon, I had watched a black and white dog while I was pet sitting at a house next to the railroad tracks. The dog seemed to be well behaved, seldom barked, and stayed with the person that I assumed was his owner. The owner was male, rough-looking, and obviously homeless since they were living under the highway bridge next to the railroad tracks.

On this August day, I decided to approach them, my curiosity and concern for the dog was getting the best of me. Besides, how bad could he be? He owned a dog. As I crossed the railroad tracks, I yelled out to them. The dog heard me and barked while tugging at his rope to come meet me, his owner following behind him. I introduced myself and said I wanted to meet his dog and see if they needed anything. The man was shy and while I was talking to him, I checked out his dog. The dog appeared to be in good condition for being on the road and I could tell the dog meant everything to the man.

I had never talked to a homeless person before. I was not sure really what to ask him. I again asked if he needed anything. He told me he did not take charity.

"I'm not offering charity; I'm asking if your dog needs anything not you," I said.

He looked at me for a few seconds before he grinned and said, "You're okay."

I explained that one of my pet sitting clients had just put his dog down that morning and he had asked me to come and get the dog's items to donate to someone who could use them. I had a new bag of dog food and treats for his dog if he would take them. He looked at his dog and pondered for a minute and then agreed to take the food.

As I walked to my vehicle to get the food and treats for his dog, I remembered I had three raincoats in my vehicle and that I only could wear one at a time. Grabbing one of them, I walked back across the railroad tracks to where they were sitting under the bridge. I set the dog food down along with the dog treats and then handed him the raincoat.

He looked at me and I said, "The coat is not for you; it's to help keep your dog dry." He smiled and took the coat.

I left there and continued along my pet-sitting route. At my next stop, I checked my phone. The man whose dog had died had posted something about his dog. I commented on his post that the items he had given me had gone to good use. I explained that I'd given them to a dog and homeless man who were living under the highway bridge.

The next day I received a call from a young woman from the newspaper office. Her coworker had seen my post on Facebook and suggested she investigate it. She asked me if I would take her to meet this man and his dog. I said I would, but I couldn't promise that he would talk to her. I also suggested she not give anything to him. I told her she could only give things to his dog because he didn't take charity.

We met as planned and both walked across the tracks. The dog was watching us from his perch. He barked as we approached, his tail wagging. His owner got up. As I greeted him, I introduced the young reporter. She explained that if he was interested, she would like to get his story for an article she was writing for the paper. To my surprise, he said yes. When the interview was over, she handed him a sleeping bag. She told him it was for his dog. The man was smiling and shaking his head as we walked away.

During the interview, we found out that his birthday would be in two days and he would be turning thirty-five; he had been on the road for seven years. His dog had been with him for four years and they had been together since the dog was a puppy. The interview came out the next week and that was the beginning of change for him and his dog.

The article in the paper went statewide, on public radio, Facebook, and more. Everyone was willing to help. He was getting stopped on the street and I was getting calls and texts from people wanting to help in all ways. There was a GoFundMe account set up for him and within three days, there were over five thousand dollars in it. He qualified for a housing program and received help getting his legal identification card, birth certificate, and medications. There were some ups and downs, but since then he has been sober for five months and is working in an employment program. He has been in contact with his sister who thought he had died on the road. She believed that he was possibly a John Doe in some morgue somewhere. After the article was published, local churches and community groups got together and started addressing the situation with the homeless teens in the area, which was a problem that no one knew about until the article began a conversation about homelessness.

It only takes one person to step up and create change. When someone does step up, they can create an impact that keeps moving and spreading like ripples from a stone tossed in the water. Will you be that person?

GEORGIA NAGEL is an animal communicator and sacred activist. She lives, breathes, and shares the sacred connectedness between our spirit and the earth. Her personal journey has been intertwined with animals, nature, and earth wisdom. She believes that if we would share the unconditional love from animals and nature, apply it to those we encounter, we will together shine a brighter light upon this world.

Georgia has authored two books; *Pet Talker: Listening to Those Who Speak Silently* and *Maurice the Goat Finds His Real Family*.

Connect with Georgia
Website: georgianagel.com
Email: gnagel@arvig.net

Week 9

Kindness in words creates confidence.
Kindness in thinking creates profoundness.
Kindness in giving creates love.

~ Lao Tzu

I CHOOSE KINDNESS

From its beginning, a morning is a compilation of tiny decisions that set the tone for the day. We awaken to a preferred alarm clock or prefer no alarm clock at all. Should we meditate or pray? Leap headfirst into exercise or lounge in bed? Oh wait, coffee versus tea? Do we walk to work/school, ride a bike, or carpool? Adding up the physical exercise we do each morning can have a big impact on our health in the long run. Similarly, if we start our days with a kind or positive mindset, it makes a big difference as we come in contact with many people *throughout* our day, week, month. If we choose these small exercises in kindness, they mold and shape our days, our weeks, our years, and truly our lives.

An old adage states, "Small hinges can move big doors." This is evident when it comes to kindness. This quote reminds us that multiple little actions can add up to larger trends. As an actuality, a tiny moment of kindness may seem ridiculously small to you, and yet it has the potentiality to be incalculably great on the receiver's end. There is always a quick and perhaps seemingly small *choice* to start this chain of events, to spark kindness, gentleness, and less judgement. Because these choices build upon one another in a positive way, the small 'hinge' of kindness can have an enormous ripple effect.

Why should we choose kindness? How does kindness really make us feel? The moment that love or kindness happens, it should be without effort or need for recognition. It should happen with spontaneity, and honor the giver and receiver. Both should feel warm and good. This is a quiet and elementary good like a hot cup of hot cocoa, a fluffy red sweater, a big hug. It is like getting a "warm fuzzy" at school when we were young.

If we go a step further to help a friend in need, we feel more profoundly good. We feel the light or peace that helps us know our true selves. Our souls are constantly expanding or transforming when we are practicing kindness on a frequent basis. Walls between us start to recede; judgement and fear fall away to strength and love.

I believe the opposite of those little "warm fuzzies" at school were called "cold pricklies." The sound of this phrase as it rolls off the tongue even feels different. Why do we want to be cold or prickly or hurtful? Unfortunately, these urges pop up. Sometimes they do so automatically, and yet thankfully we get to *choose* to remedy them. Deciding to right a wrong is only a slight detour in the overall scheme of living with a kind heart. With patience and practice, we begin to lean toward more kindness, more often. We can also choose how we respond when a cold prickly happens or a hurtful event occurs. The way we react defines what type of person we are. There is healing in forgiveness and coming from a place of sincere love is not only a part of our evolution, but often feels the best to both the forgiver as well as to the person that is being forgiven. Life on earth is unpredictable; our everyday fates are unknown, and hardships inevitably happen. Let people off that proverbial hook.

Many people often help us feel warm, invited, and supported. That leads us to then feel true connection with them. Connection is uplifting, joyful, and often craved as a basic human need. Connection to God/Source/Universe/Spirit is profound and fulfilling and it lights us up. Connections to other humans do as well. The power of spiritual and human connections is strong and yet palpable. Remember to stay close to the people or connections that help perpetuate kindness. These connections in our lives are truly meaningful.

My father was a family practice physician for over forty years. He was a warm, supportive man with an indescribably inviting aura that magnetized people towards him. His former patients still talk about his kind and giving ways, which left many of them wishing he could have continued practicing medicine forever. I have heard some of them say that his presence in their lives was truly meaningful. What is amazing is that my father usually only met with a patient for thirty minutes, maybe an hour at one time, a couple times a year. Yet the reach of his kindness was enormous. It was not only that he was intuitive and knowledgeable, but it was the *feeling* that he gave people that brought them back and kept them talking about him years after their last appointment.

He passed away last year and writing this gives me the chance to acknowledge him and marvel at his impact in our community. I feel so lucky to have witnessed his example, to be given the chance to follow in his footsteps and *choose* to give people that same feeling of receptivity, true listening, understanding, and love.

I choose to use small actions to create big change. I choose connection and I choose kindness. Let us all spread kindness. Let us continuously shift towards ease and warmth and support for each other. This *can* become a more beautiful world that I would be proud to have helped create.

Just like I choose to have my coffee first in the morning before meditation, I choose kindness.

I choose kindness.

HEATHER WALKER is a Physician Assistant (PA) in women's health and has been practicing for over fifteen years, helping women feel better physically, mentally, and emotionally with a focus on whole body health. She also is a kindness crusader and is using relationship marketing to help others spread kindness to both current and future personal and business relationships.

Send a kindness card (make it digitally & then it is stamped, sealed and mailed in the USPS mail!): bit.ly/Choosingkindness

Connect with Heather
Email: Hwalker@email.com
Facebook: Heather Locke Walker
LinkedIn: linkedin.com/in/heatherwalkerpa

Week 10

Kindness is the language which the deaf can hear and the blind can see.

~ Mark Twain

IT'S THE LITTLE THINGS – A KINDNESS STORY

Sometimes it seems as though all I have done in the last ten years is cry. I was pushed to my limits by my husband's illness and death, the loss of our house, our possessions, and our animals to a devastating fire; an across-the-state move; retiring after an almost fifty-year nursing career and missing it dearly; plus, developing an immune-system illness that limits my mobility and causes much pain. These were all huge things over which I mostly did not have control. Even so, as I learned to cope with the big changes, it became the little things that helped me to *continue anyway* and that offered a small aspect of control to my life. Of all these little things, kindness helps so much. Small kindnesses may be just the things that keep the weary soul from giving in to the pressure of grief or stress or hopelessness. A little kindness goes a long way. Here is a little example.

The roar of the plane droned into the night as the bright midnight sun of Alaska turned into the darkness of the midwestern sky. The lights were dimmed in the quiet cabin for the red-eye flight. Many of the travelers dozed as the soft movements of the plane rocked them. It mimicked the rocking motion of my grandmother's old chair in the front room of my childhood home. I found it soothing and comforting. Soft snores emitted from the seat behind me where a young couple snuggled together.

When I boarded the plane, the woman in the couple had said, "Here let me help you with that, it looks heavy." Taking my bag, she carried it to my seat. It was a little kindness that went a long way.

The plane's cabin was only half full and the cabin crew allowed all of us to spread out. I had been able to curl my weary body up across three seats and using my newly purchased neck-support pillow as a headrest, I had gotten somewhat comfortable. The steward's thoughtful kindness went a long way.

Alaska is a long distance from Illinois and traveling alone was stressful for me but arriving alone at midnight in an almost empty airport was even more so. My immune system illness caused me to not be able to walk well. This was especially true after two back-to-back long flights.

The baggage claim was a good distance away. I hesitated to ask for help, knowing there were those who might need it more. Waiting as I deboarded was a skinny African American kid. He looked like a teenager. Settling me into a wheelchair, he pushed me up the ramp from the plane to the airport. He must have been stronger than he looked. The entire time he kept up chatter with me about the trip and how he would help me. But first, he had to check on another passenger. He asked if I would mind waiting.

"Of course not," I said.

I had noted the rather confused-looking man with a bruised face, blackened eye, and arm in a sling. He was sitting with his family as we waited to board our flight. They had been seated in the front seats of the first-class section.

My helper parked me and ran off to get the other passenger with the bruised face. The man's family were hovering and told the young helper they would take their dad to the bathroom and they could manage. The kid was insistent that he help them.

"No. No. No," they said.

They insisted that they could do it.

They pointed in my direction and said, "Help her."

It was another little kindness.

Hesitantly, the kid began to push me toward the baggage claim, all the while muttering about it not being safe for them to try to take him alone. Didn't they know he could fall? He wished they would have let him help.

As it often happens, the passengers arrived before the bags. My helper leaned over and asked if it would be okay for him to go check on the family with the injured man. He sprinted off toward the bathroom. He was showing another little kindness.

As I waited for the bags, the baggage began to come up on the opposite carousel from where we had been told to expect them. I was facing backward, and the chair locked from the back. I could not see what was happening. As I was trying to stand and turn around, the young woman from earlier came over and turned the chair so that I could watch for my bag. It was another little kindness.

Before I knew it, the kid was back. He was pushing the injured man as he helped get them settled to receive their bags. He then came to me. I pointed out my bag. He grabbed it and off we went.

I will be taking you to your car ma'am, do you remember where it is parked?" he asked.

Amazingly, I did.

A few minutes later, we had traversed another ramp, several sidewalk bumps, and a curb. I found myself sitting by my car. He opened the tailgate, tossed in my bag, made sure I got in the car and that it started. He then told me it was a pleasure to help me and I should drive very carefully home. It was a final little kindness.

His little kindnesses in making the end of my trip go smoothly went a long way to help this very tired grandmother who had just traveled a few thousand miles and still had a three-hour drive to complete the trip home.

I thanked him for being so kind, told him how much I appreciated him, his thoughtfulness, and his help, and I tipped him well. My little kindness.

This story illustrates how in just a few simple actions we can make one another's lives go more smoothly. As we become Kindness Crusaders, let's keep this our thought for the week and always, "Touching lives, touching hearts, spreading kindness."

MARGARET-MAGGIE HONNOLD writes based on her life as a registered nurse, health educator, widow, mother, grandmother, and former Alzheimer's caregiver. Graduating from Kankakee Community College and Eastern Illinois University with degrees in nursing and health education, her experience in hospital and community settings allows her to write insightfully into life's circumstances.

She's a volunteer church elder and board member for the Kibbe Historical Museum, and Hearts of Hancock Humane Society. Her favorite thing is to cuddle with her two basset hounds, and bloodhound puppy, and to take her camera, wander the countryside photographing her beloved Mississippi River and the mid-west landscape.

Connect with Margaret-Maggie
Website: margarethonnold.com
Website: theartofcontinuinganyway.godaddysites.com
Email: machonnold@outlook.com
Facebook: margarethonnold

Week 11

Talk to yourself like you would to someone you love.

~ Brené Brown

BECOMING YOUR BFF

Most of us enter adulthood shaped by family values. Through cumulative life experiences our perceptions may change, redefining our personal values and creating different aspirations.

Early in life, I developed a negative self-image and poor self-esteem. My mother was critical of my weight, clothing choices, grades, who I dated, career considerations. She could diminish my self-worth with a harsh tongue lashing or by embarrassing me in front of others. It took me years to find the courage to tell my mother that I was majoring in animal science (against her advice) and planned to become a veterinarian. Before she went into her bedroom to cry, her only question was what I would do if I didn't get into veterinary school?

My confidence was bolstered after I gained experience with a veterinarian, earned a Bachelor of Science degree, magna cum laude, worked in cancer research, and received co-author credits on research publications. I was admitted to Texas A&M's College of Veterinary Medicine but felt devastated when being there never felt right and I struggled to understand why. After considerable reflection, I recognized that the "journey" to get into vet school was more important than my arrival at the "destination". I left A&M. Achieving balance between my professional and personal lives became a priority. I went on to train as a physician assistant and perfusionist. Working as a perfusionist proved frustrating. Abusive and unprofessional behavior by powerful cardiovascular surgeons was condoned. The surgeons' attitudes trickled down to other operating room professions. Due to a lack of career satisfaction, I shifted to my career as a physician assistant. I began working at a local hospital. I was blessed with supportive supervisors and caring colleagues. I was rewarded by patients' expressions of gratitude and career advancement. More than twenty years later, I still find fulfillment working in the same setting.

Feeling successful in my personal life was more elusive. Over time my mother's role in shaping poor relationship choices became clear. She had three marriages ending in divorce and had several volatile relationships interspersed between them. Mom was unhappy, bitter, angry, and increasingly fearful of being alone. I made personal changes, hoping to avoid her fate. Later I met a man of which we shared similar interests and goals. I was drawn to his close and loving family. We were married and had one son. The outer trappings of success hid residual inner insecurities and self-criticism. My psyche was damaged further when my husband and son began siding against me. I felt disrespected and like an outsider in my own home. I grappled with voicing my opinions and concerns to my husband. Our marriage withered and our efforts to repair it were unsuccessful. I was conflicted about staying in a marriage devoid of intimacy versus leaving, potentially risking financial stability as well as estrangement from my son.

The universe sent several strong messages to me in 2014. A toxic new supervisor wreaked havoc in my department (his removal took a year). My mother's dementia worsened, but she resisted entering assisted living. My mother-in-law was diagnosed with metastatic brain cancer, dying less than two months later. My son, who had been awarded a four-year scholarship, teetered on failing out of college. My beloved twenty-seven-year-old horse, who had been with me longer than my husband, had declining health and I needed to decide what was in his best interest.

I sought clarity wherever I could to help me understand the universe's message(s). I practiced yoga, meditation and mindfulness. I journaled and attended workshops on vision boarding and Sanskrit mantras. I went to Oprah's *Live Your Best Life* and a Brené Brown workshop on The *Gifts of Imperfection*. I read Deepak Chopra's *Seven Sacred Laws for Spiritual Success* at a beachfront yoga retreat. I attended NVC training, breath work classes, and biofield tuning sessions. Participation in Celebrate Your Life sessions, webinars with Sunny Dawn Johnston and Mindvalley, and a Sedona retreat led to more valuable insights.

Gradually, I became more present and learned I was the cause of my own suffering and the only one who could cure it. Oprah reminded me that I increased my suffering by ignoring messages from the universe. A fellow workshop participant taught me I wasn't "broken" and didn't need to be "fixed". I finally appreciated how powerful my words were. I began tolerating my flaws. Learning that negative self-talk is a form of self-violence led me to pay attention to my internal dialogue, use kinder language towards myself, and accept my imperfections. The concepts of abundance, identifying life desires and finding my dharma resonated with me. As my clarity grew, I realized my biggest dilemma; I had been thinking with my head instead of feeling with my heart. This a-ha moment pointed me down the right path. I acknowledged the good I had shared with my husband and the mistakes we made that caused the deterioration of our marriage. I understood why I struggled with deciding. I released my anger and accepted our efforts to renew our marriage had failed. It was time to move out and move on.

Soon I began manifesting some of my desires. The more I embraced change and generosity, the more gratitude and joy I experienced. I felt secure personally and financially. I wasn't afraid of being on my own or expressing my authenticity. I reached an equitable settlement with my ex-husband to finalize our divorce.

I was finally thriving - not just surviving!

Later I participated in a webinar focusing on being our own best-friend-forever (BFF). We talked about needing self-care, giving ourselves permission to be flawed, and forgiving ourselves for mistakes. We discussed ways we treat and honor our closest friends. We were encouraged to acknowledge mistreatment of our own BFFs (our bodies), apologize, and make amends. This message resonated with me. I remembered the critical and self-loathing language I used for years. I was proud that I replaced it with kindness and accepted this person I saw in the mirror as imperfectly beautiful and loving regardless of what size she wore. My BFF was doing the best she could.

Passing by a mirror while reflecting on my BFF, a sudden realization hit me. I was unkind to myself every time, I hid my body by wearing a shawl or avoiding the pool while in my swimsuit. Tears trickled down my cheeks and profound sadness filled me. I wasn't being my own BFF unconditionally! I would never be ashamed and demean a close friend this way. I'd point out her positive features, tell her she is beautiful inside and out, and help her embrace her unique self (including her imperfections). I apologized for being oblivious to the cruelty I inflicted over the years. I thanked my BFF for giving me legs strong enough to ride horses and hike through forests, eyes that showed me all the beauty and wonder in our world, a sparkling smile capable of lighting up someone's day. I told my BFF I embraced her for being as she was meant to be. I promised my BFF that I'd show more gratitude for her attributes and be more mindful of judging her flaws.

The journey continues for me and my BFF. I am respectful and proud of my BFF. I strive to give her the love and kindness she deserves. She forgives me unconditionally when I falter. Together we are thriving!

DEBBIE TODD lives in Houston, Texas, where she enjoys a career as a physician assistant. She has nearly thirty years of experience in medical, surgical and psychiatric specialties. Her interest in alternative medicine grew while providing traditional medical care. Debbie embraces using a holistic approach to healthcare in her personal and professional life.

Debbie's interests include gardening, making malas (and other jewelry), enjoying nature and being a lifelong learner. Her aspirations include traveling more, authoring books and spreading kindness.

Connect with Debbie
Email: findingzentoo@gmail.com
Email: marvelousmalasandmore@gmail.com

Week 12

*Kindness makes you the most beautiful person
in the world, no matter what you look like.*

~ Anonymous

A STURDY CONTAINER OF LIGHT

I have a tendency to be super nice. I now know that being nice is not quite as special as I used to think it was. I used to fill with pride when someone told me that I was nice. In fact, many people said that I was one of the nicest people they had ever known.

Those comments led to questions. If I was so nice, then why was I never enough? Why were my feelings disregarded, my emotions not allowed, and my spirit lacking joy?

I spent a lot of time feeling sad, hurt, angry, and lonely. I did not know how to say no. I deeply needed to fit in by being liked and thought of as special. This need compelled me to stay in the cycle of shame that I now call, *Niceness*.

When I used to be nice, I allowed myself to be disrespected by friends, family members, clients, and neighbors. For example, I had two clients that were a married couple. They would ask me to do extra things for them. They'd ask me to type out lesson details after they took a horseback riding class. They said this was because they would forget what to practice in between lessons. I would not be compensated for this extra time. These same clients would cancel lessons with less than twenty-four-hours' notice. I continually failed to charge them for the late cancellation as per my policy.

I had no concept of boundaries, but I noticed that I felt bad around these people most of the time. I wondered why they wanted so much from me, and I built up resentments towards them that leaked out passive aggressively. I imagined us as bumblebees buzzing around together and stinging each other when one bumped into one another.

I wasn't sleeping well due to the stress of pushing myself beyond my limits. I was working twelve-hour days, six or seven days a week, and semi-functioning on four hours of sleep. Self-care was something I knew nothing about back when I was being a nice people-pleaser. However, I was painfully aware that lack of sleep made me less than patient at times. My anxiety was out of control and I felt edgy. This edginess affected my family because I was so preoccupied with all I had to do that I had trouble focusing on their needs. It's strange how a person can go through life, living in their mind and body every day, but not really knowing what is happening around them and to them because of their own choices and behaviors. I might very well still be in this cycle if not for a tremendous shift in my world that would forever change me.

Little did I know that after a lifetime of trying to be nice and still never feeling appreciated, a series of traumas would emotionally and physically shatter me. I was like a glass of water breaking into tiny pieces as the callous ground rose to meet it. Freefalling in darkness, I found nothing familiar to grab hold of. Pain ripped through every fiber of my being and I was sure I would die from it.

On a particularly bleak day, I was feeling lost in despair and decided to take a long hike on a rugged desert trail that I had never hiked before. Dark thoughts were festering in my mind as I struggled to find my way through unfamiliar terrain. I began to suspect that I was lost. I barely noticed that my shins were bleeding from wading through thick sticker branches. As the sky darkened to dusk, I felt sure I would spend the night out there when suddenly, from out of nowhere a ray of light miraculously showed itself in the form of a hand shaped by kindness. I grabbed hold of it. In that moment, I felt that there were two choices for me. One choice was to move away from this ray of hope and slide back into the darkness so it could take me from this world. The other choice whispered that I should find the will to stand up and take the first step, scary as it seemed, into a new existence.

I have a feeling that the light revealed itself to me because I have more to do here in this place. The path of transformation into my own power has been arduous, wild, terrible, beautiful, and freeing. Throughout this journey, I've felt the light growing within myself, filling up every nook and cranny until a calm peaceful center has been formed. From this peaceful center, I intuited that this light led me to kindness. I learned that practicing self-kindness was not selfish and I needed to be kind to myself in order to heal. One of the first things I did was to get centered and determine what I wanted my life to look like. To achieve some of those goals, I had to learn to set boundaries so I would be less likely to fall back into people pleasing. Boundaries also needed to be set with those that I had allowed to take advantage of me. These needed to be clearly stated along with consequences for stepping over the boundaries that I had set.

One boundary I created with the clients mentioned earlier was that they would need to take notes or videotape their riding lessons so that they could refer to it. I would no longer be writing the lessons out for them unless they wanted to pay for the extra time in advance. They said that they would do this and did one time. The very next lesson, they tried to bully and guilt me into continuing as I had before. I held firm, but they treated me in a disrespectful manner. I let them know that I would not work with them unless they apologized and agreed not to do this again. They refused. I let them know I would no longer teach them. It was scary to do this, and I was quite shook up over it, but I was so proud of that act of kindness that I had gifted myself by standing in my own power.

Over time and with lots of practice, it became easier to kindly care for myself. It became easier to kindly refuse to do things that didn't align with my values. Space began to free up for more of what I wanted to spend my time on. Passion projects opened before me. Joy began to ring in my heart. I discovered new internal energy.

I wondered what was igniting so much abundance in my life. I explored this question with patient curiosity. When the flower of that curiosity finally bloomed, it was kindness that unfolded.

I am a sturdy container of light.

Kindness is holding the light for yourself and others. It's not about agreeing to everything or fitting in. It's about belonging to yourself first and then belonging in the world where people are attracted to you because you are authentically you. Authenticity emanates from a place of kindness. In this space, we can see all the possibilities life has to offer. We are able to step into that space, take a deep breath, and move forward with love, hope, and passion. By granting myself permission to shift from being nice to being kind, I found my power. I have become a sturdy container of light that holds the potential of kindness for others. May the light of kindness also fill you.

DARCIE LITWICKI works as a life coach and offers equine-assisted awareness to women. She is the owner of Silver Heart Ranch, LLC, located in Vail, Arizona.

Darcie observed how coaching tapped into helping women realize their authenticity and power. She is passionate about bringing women and horses together in an experiential process that includes life coaching and work with horses to deepen the process of inner self-work that leads to women stepping into their own power.

Her clients are moving forward with strength and positivity for the betterment of their communities and future generations.

Please visit her website to learn more about her programs.

Connect with Darcie
Website: silverheartranch.com
Email: darcielitwicki@gmail.com

Week 13

Kindness is more important than wisdom, and the recognition of this is the beginning of wisdom.

~ Theodore Isaac Rubin

LIFE LESSONS OF KINDNESS

My family embarked on a journey to the Grand Canyon, one of many road trips we took years ago. Just five hours into our adventure, our old station wagon gave out on the highway. This was long before cellphones. Just as we were sitting there wondering what we were going to do, a tow truck pulled up and a man asked if we needed help. He offered to tow us to his garage and "take a look" at the car. We decided to put our trust into him and the five of us piled into his truck and drove to his place of business.

Sure enough, it was the transmission that had died. He said he would order the parts needed and start to rebuild it as soon as he could. You can imagine the thoughts that were running through our minds. We were trusting him to know what he was doing. We worried about how much this would cost and about being at his mercy.

Because it was Saturday, he couldn't get the parts until Monday. We would be spending three days in Bettendorf, Iowa. We started talking about renting a car and must have looked forlorn. He offered us a car to use for free for the weekend. We were surprised and offered him money, which he refused. Feeling quite sad about this turn of events on our grand trip but grateful for a car, we took off to check into a motel. It was one which he had recommended. We were trusting him again.

During the next two days, we visited a couple of parks, tried to see what a casino boat with gambling looked like, but were refused entrance due to having children, and did some other sightseeing including the city zoo. We happened to arrive on the day of the oldest elephant celebrating his thirtieth birthday. Local press, flashing cameras, and tourists were everywhere. Our kids thought it was just great. Later, watching the ten o'clock news in our room, we were able to enjoy the elephant's birthday experience again.

On Monday afternoon, we picked up our car hoping that all would be well. After paying for the job and thanking him profusely for his timeliness, generosity, and kindness, we took off for our destination.

He made such an impression that we still talk about the kindness of this man and the lesson of trust that we learned from him.

Maybe it was through putting my faith in a stranger that led me to repay the favor years later. I was driving in a small town and on my way to a metaphysical store to offer my services. As I pulled up to a stop sign, a woman came to my car window asking for money for her and her granddaughter. She said she had been evicted from her apartment and just needed some money for groceries. She pointed to the bushes over in the park and sure enough, there was a young girl around eight. I pulled over to get out of the way of traffic. She hung onto my car door and kept talking, continuing to tell me the full story of what happened. She actually needed sixty dollars to pay her landlord in order to get back into her apartment. I had been solicited by many homeless people and frequently gave a dollar or two, trying not to judge them or their circumstances, but sixty dollars was a bold request.

Admittedly, I went into full judgement mode. *Was she ripping me off? Who is that girl? This woman could be a trafficker and had stolen her! How dare she ask for that much?! She must be a drug addict. What if she hurt me? She most definitely is homeless, because sixty dollars would not cover rent. There is no apartment!*

Somehow through all my horrible judgements, I managed to look at her face and into her eyes, and I saw a traumatized soul. I told her I would drive her to the closest grocery store so she could at least buy some food. I asked her to call her granddaughter over to the car, although I didn't tell her why. I wanted to see her closeup and check for signs of fear. As soon as the girl got into the back seat of my car, I could see there was a deep sadness in her face and that the two of them were close. I felt myself letting go of my own fear and paying attention to my intuition, feeling a pang in my softening heart.

As we drove to the grocery store, she told me her daughter, the young girl's mother, was a drug addict. The court had given this grandmother custody. Then she had lost her job at a retail store. As a result, she could not pay her rent and had been evicted. She had not been able to find a job for the last few weeks; the landlord had warned her.

The whole litany of unfortunate circumstances and bad luck all started sounding plausible. More importantly, I could see the flight-or-fight response in her body, the look in her eyes that told of her fear and embarrassment. I heard the shaky sound of her voice telling her story and her anger at the world for giving her this raw deal.

By the time we arrived at the grocery store, my fear had dissolved. I felt nothing but empathy. I am not a cash-carrying person, but oddly happened to have a little over sixty dollars in my wallet that day. I gave her all of it, and then gave her my cellphone number in case of emergency, even though I lived an hour away. I told her to call me if she needed anything else. I had no idea what I would do or say if she did call.

Sometimes we do these acts of kindness and have no idea what happens once our deed is finished. Fortunately, the ending was revealed to me. The owner of the metaphysical store later told me that she knew the woman and heard that she and her granddaughter were able to move back into their apartment. I have no idea how or where she may have gotten enough money to pay rent, perhaps others were helping, but I stopped questioning. I only know that I was guided by my intuition and by the spirit telling me to let go of my judgements and just trust.

Both stories offered me an incredible life lesson in trust, a value I would not necessarily associate with kindness. To receive the mechanic's gifts of a free tow in the middle of nowhere, allowing him to take apart our transmission when we had no idea of his knowledge or experience, and then even the use of his car for free, all required a level of trust and faith.

To give money to another human being who you don't know, and has a very suspicious story, requires trust and compassion. Acts of kindness can teach us a multitude of lessons if we can open our hearts to receive those gifts.

CHRISTINE MOSES MS founder of Featherheart Holistic Paths, provides counseling and guidance for personal and spiritual growth utilizing many healing traditions and practices. She provides the facilitation of women's groups and retreats for integration of mind, body, and spirit.

Christine holds a Master of Science in Holistic Ministries, is a certified shamanic practitioner, Reiki Master, ordained interfaith minister, ceremonialist, certified retreat leader and author. She also trains other women to lead sacred circles through her inspiring book *The Wisdom of Circles: Gathering Women for Conscious Community*. She has also co-authored *52 Weeks of Gratitude Journal*.

Connect with Christine
Website: chrisfeatherheart.com
Email: christinemoses11@gmail.com
Phone: 847-525-2600

Week 14

A tree is known by its fruit; a man by his deeds. A good deed is never lost; he who sows courtesy reaps friendship and he who plants kindness gathers love.

~ Saint Basil

KINDNESS IS CLEANSING

It was thanks to a dirty load of laundry that I learned that often the most profound, touching, and selfless act of kindness is a simple gesture. We may forget the kind words or even the kind person, but we seldom forget the act and how it made us feel. This incident with dirty laundry reminded me that the power behind acts of kindness linger and warms our hearts.

I had been traveling the Greek islands for six weeks and was staying in an Airbnb on the island of Syros for three days. Although it wasn't typical for most rentals in Greece, I actually had a washer and dryer, but there was no detergent!

Beware if you travel there. The island air is intoxicating and may cause short-term memory loss, which was why I kept forgetting to buy detergent during my stay. There finally came a point though when I was in desperate need of clean clothes.

On my last night in Syros, I got off at my bus stop and began searching for a market while walking home. I was almost home and had yet to spot a market, so I was getting worried. As I approached my Airbnb, I spotted three elderly women sitting on a porch near my rental.

"Excuse me," I said as I approached them with a giant smile on my face. "Do you speak English?"

They turned towards me. Their faces were warm, loving, and graceful. They shook their heads no.

I wondered if they would know the English word "market." It seemed like a common word, so I said it out loud.

"Ah," they all sighed in unison. They started speaking over each other in Greek and became animated with their hands. I used my own hand gestures to ask if there was a market close by. One lady shook her finger no at me again.

With a hopeful tone, I explained in English that I needed laundry detergent.

Nothing.

I was becoming desperate, but I stood there calmly waiting for an answer on how to proceed.

I heard an intuitive whisper, "Charades."

I figured I had nothing to lose and began acting out "washing." I pointed to my clothes and pretended I was washing them. The lightbulb suddenly went on because one lady ran inside and came back with a bar of soap. It was not quite liquid detergent, but we were making progress!

We stood there in silence for a few moments simply staring at each other. To break the silence, one lady started a language lesson and began pointing to random articles of clothing. She had me repeat what she was saying in Greek. This lightened our mood of desperation as we all giggled at my inability to speak Greek with as much grace and ease as they could.

Then the lightbulb went on for me. I went to the Google Translate app on my phone and typed in, "washing machine."

I showed it to them.

"Ah," they all said.

A door slammed and another neighbor came out into the street. One of the women called her over and to my surprise, she spoke English!

I explained that I was leaving the next day and needed laundry detergent. The next thing I knew she told me to grab a cup, turned around, and gracefully went back inside her house with no explanation. To my surprise, she returned carrying liquid laundry detergent!

Yes! My heart was overpouring with gratitude and joy for this Greek angel who came out of nowhere and delivered what I asked for. I call her an angel because she literally disappeared into the horizon just as quickly as she appeared.

I stood there for a moment relishing in the beauty of this experience and how one cup of laundry detergent had the power to create a surge of positive energy that radiated throughout my entire body. I was also in awe of the kindness of these complete strangers who were so determined to help a desperate American traveler.

Before I left the island, I felt compelled to express my gratitude, so I purchased a box of candy and wrote a thank-you card in Greek. One of my friends assisted me with that.

With my bags packed, I walked over to one of the neighbors who helped and handed her the gift. I could tell by her facial expression that she was shocked at my gesture. She started speaking in Greek and had an angelic expression of appreciation on her face. I slowly reached for her hand and then brought my other hand to my heart.

"Thank you," I said in a grateful tone.

Time stood still as we stared into the depths of each other's souls, smiles on our faces.

"Café?" she asked suddenly to break the silence.

She was inviting me in for coffee, but I politely declined as my ride was on the way.

She continued to speak Greek and then yelled loudly. One of the women who had helped appeared and walked over towards us. She saw the box of candies and had a look of surprise on her face as well. She kissed me on both of my cheeks as she spoke cheerful words in her beautiful language. Another kiss happened as I held my heart again, expressing utmost gratitude for our casual encounter.

As I was driving away, I could not stop rewinding this sacred exchange and smiling. I was in awe of the kindness these elderly women had towards a complete stranger. They reminded me of the healing power of presence. We don't need to speak the same language in order to show kindness towards another, and it does not require much effort; we just need to show up with an open and loving heart.

A compassionate heart of someone who gives with no expectations of receiving in return has the capacity to permeate and amplify a random act of kindness. These women were simply giving from the kindness of their hearts and I quickly realized that kindness is limitless!

When we show up fully in our actions towards others, we actively co-create a universe full of kindness and giving with every choice that we make. Never underestimate how the smallest and simplest gestures have the power to bring a smile and light to an unpleasant situation or how the effects of kindness can extend far beyond a given moment.

Giving is its own reward. It activates the light within us as it reaches out and activates the light in others, which in turn inspires love and connection. The ripple effect amplifies the collective consciousness of the world.

A simple act of kindness is accessible to all and it's a simple choice we mindfully make. Our choice to connect with others through kindness has the power to change another's day, which can make the journey for all more enjoyable and fulfilling. I will never underestimate the power of a single gesture of kindness after this experience.

My Greek angels will forever be my lingering reminder of kindness.

LIBBY RAPIN is a mindset coach, speaker, and the founder of Something Beautiful. Her life mission is to bring healing to the world by helping people experience more joy, love, and fulfillment through mindfulness. She is based in Saginaw, Michigan, but can oftentimes be found frolicking all over the world, feeding her soul with spontaneous travel adventures.

Libby is the podcast host of *Light as A Feather* and co-creator of the YouTube video series, *Oh, Infinite Love.*

You can stay up to date on Libby's work and travel adventures by following her on social media or visiting her website.

Connect with Libby
Website: somethingbeautiful.co
Facebook: itissomethingbeautiful
Instagram: itissomethingbeautiful
YouTube Channel: Oh, Infinite Love
Podcast: w4divas.com/hosts/libby-rapin

Week 15

This is my simple religion. There is no need for temples; no need for complicated philosophy. Our own brain, our own heart is our temple; the philosophy is kindness.

~ Dalai Lama

ACCEPTING GRACE

If you've ever been the recipient of an act of kindness, then you know how amazing it feels. It's also an incredible experience to pay it forward. Think back recently. Did opportunities present themselves to be kind or to accept someone's grace? Did you take advantage of a situation to either give or receive? Kindness is sometimes hard to accept, yet easy to provide, and it comes in all shapes and sizes. It could be as simple as a friendly smile at a stranger or a bigger investment such as offering to help your neighbor move.

The mystery for many is why accepting grace is more difficult than giving it from your heart? From my experience, it always feels good to sprinkle kindness and compassion. Still it somehow feels selfish accepting it in return. However, I've learned that we all deserve to feel the joy of giving. Just as importantly, we also deserve to feel the grace of receiving.

A few years ago, my best friend and I decided we would participate in the National Random Acts of Kindness Day. We didn't have a plan but knew we wanted to commit to several small random acts of kindness sprinkled throughout our community. Within a few hours, we had spread joy wherever the adventure guided us, which was a magical feeling like none other. Seeing the delight and appreciation on the faces of strangers was humbling; giving so little meant so much. We were surprised at some reactions, which often brought us to tears.

A young couple squealed in delight as we offered a small token. It was as if they had won the lottery or something much greater than we provided. They enthusiastically said that they would be passing the kindness on. Their reaction was the true meaning of accepting grace and then paying it forward. We spotted an elderly woman shopping at a discount grocery store and as she was reaching into her wallet, we offered the payment to the clerk. The shopper misunderstood and tried to pay us back. When we explained our mission for the day, tears formed in her eyes as she couldn't believe someone would do that for her. We witnessed her acceptance of grace from two strangers that she most likely would never come across again. We had ear-to-ear smiles when we saw someone paying it forward when they didn't see us watching.

Some of the small acts of kindness we provided that day were buying groceries; paying for a bus fare and toll for the person driving behind us; buying coffee for police officers as well as for the car behind us in line at a drive-thru; and giving gift cards to a young couple that randomly passed us on the sidewalk; giving gift cards to another man in line at a local shop; and dropping off bakery-made butter cookies the shop was famous for to the hair salon we both frequented. Each time we showed kindness, the recipients were thankful and surprised. We may have only done a few random acts of kindness that day, but what was given back to us was tenfold. Our souls were fed, and our hearts were full. I've often wondered about those people we met that Saturday, and my hope is we made an impact on their lives in a way that continued a string of kindness. It was a day I'll never forget, which brings me to another story that I'll always remember; I was the recipient of an act of kindness.

At the time, I was a stay-at-home mom and my husband had lost his job. I didn't seek employment since our number one priority was raising children at home and my husband expected to return to work within a short time. Money was tight and we didn't have enough groceries to make it through to the next unemployment check and felt desperate. Thinking back, we never considered getting state aid. Maybe that was out of pride; but my husband and I wanted to be able to provide for our children.

I remember a dear friend had phoned and she heard the struggle in my voice. I reluctantly revealed my concerns about money and not being able to buy groceries. She offered to bring me a few things and immediately I said no. Compassionately, she explained she didn't mind and would be happy to bring a few basics. After realizing what an act of kindness she was offering, I let down my guard and graciously accepted. I gave her a small list of things to get us by. That afternoon, she appeared at my door with not one bag of groceries but two that were heaping full. Groceries were piled past the rim of the brown, paper bags. Tears immediately billowed in my eyes and began to flow like an unstoppable dam. It was a happy and humbling moment for me. She unselfishly thought about what she would buy for our family and blessed me with her love, kindness, grace, and bountiful offering. The kindness and love that poured from her heart into mine connected us both as friends, mothers, and women.

You never know what tomorrow holds. That day we not only celebrated our friendship and our faith, but we also celebrated our love for our families and the importance of being a mother. She blessed my family that day and made us feel loved, appreciated, and supported. This story has been on my heart for years and I'd wondered if my dear friend remembered her act of kindness. Because I'm sharing this story, I've reached out reminding her of the day and how much her grace meant to me.

Kindness is one of the greatest things we can give and receive. Acts of kindness and accepting grace change us in ways we could never imagine; it opens our heart and shines light and love into our souls. Always be kind. You never know what your neighbor, friend, or even the stranger sitting next to you might be going through. Whether you're being kind or accepting grace, it will always attract more into your life. Let's see how much love we can create; cast some goodness into the universe and watch the ripple effect unfold.

Use the monthly calendars to inspire your imagination and sprinkle kindness wherever life leads you and remember to accept any grace along the way. Both will be life changing.

Blessings of kindness.

SHERYL GOODWIN MAGIERA founder of Imperfectly Charming, is a certified life coach, writer, facilitator of women's retreats and workshops. A former corporate/international trainer connects women to their hearts, uncovering who they were created to be. Sheryl provides heart-centered guidance filled with humor and love to support their journeys. She loves yoga, the outdoors, writing, reading, adventure and spending time with family and friends. She's honored to support your path of discovery; it's time to step into your light and shine.

Connect with your heart and Sheryl's to schedule a complimentary discovery session on uncovering your soul's purpose. Download her free worksheet to get started living on purpose.

Connect with Sheryl
Website: ImperfectlyCharming.com
Email: ImperfectlyCharming@gmail.com
Phone: 847-399-7775

Week 16

Goodness is about character - integrity, honesty, kindness, generosity, moral courage, and the like. More than anything else, it is about how we treat other people.

~ Dennis Prager

THROUGH TRAGEDY, KINDNESS
CAN BE YOUR BIGGEST BLESSING!

It was 2006 and life was good. Both my husband and I were on the same road to recovery and were emotionally, physically, and spiritually healing. We had been married for ten years and life was getting better and better. My husband had been through some pretty tough health challenges that year.

We decided that the Veterans Administration Hospital would be the best option for him, and our healing journey continued. The care he received there was outstanding. He was getting stronger and stronger. His nurse was an exceptional person always taking time with us and making sure we did not have any questions. She was a true angel in the hospital and a very special person to us both.

The hospital was about three hours from our home, so our weekends were important to us. Healing our lives and marriage and mending our family relations was all at the top of our to-do lists. We were on the same journey. We believed that God was first, and our spiritual growth was amazing.

My husband had been complaining of a new pain in his lower back and legs. It was Labor Day weekend and we spent the most incredible weekend together. We journeyed to our daughter's (my stepdaughter) home and stayed at a hotel. We had our grand girls stay with us as we overtook the hotel, swimming and barbequing. I normally do not splurge, but we got an amazing suite, so we had plenty of room. Our daughter made us a lunch that was her dad's favorite. He even had an opportunity to speak to his former wife and make amends for the past.

We swam with the family on the last night at the hotel and he asked me to tell them his story about his spiritual experience that he'd had. My reply was that this was his story and he got the honor of telling it. He told them about the dream he had where he'd been walking on the beach with his maker. He explained how in the dream there had been an overwhelming sense of forgiveness and unconditional love, which he now carried with him every day. He was in the best place ever in his life.

It was one of the most memorable weekends ever. We had one more night as we drove back to the hospital. That night we stayed in a nice hotel. I went out and got him one of his favorite pies and we stayed up talking and laughing. Our favorite prayer was the "St. Francis of Assisi" and at one point we both said out loud, "I get it! It's better to love than to be loved."

This was a magical moment in our marriage.

The next day I dropped him off early at the hospital and hugged him and cried. We were planning on him coming home and being done with his care in fifty more days. I had the hardest time leaving him that early morning. I was crying all the way back home as I was thinking of the amazing weekend we just had. I thought about how it just couldn't get any better than this.

We talked that night on the phone about how we were helping others and how that helped us both. We ended the conversation with, "I love you."

"I love you more."

"No, I do."

That night I had some friends at the house, and I got a call from the Chaplin of the hospital telling me my husband had been in an accident. He was in surgery and that the surgeon would be calling me, but I should probably come right away.

He'd been returning to the hospital on his bicycle. He'd just dropped off pictures of the weekend to get developed. He was hit from behind.

My heart sank. I slid down the wall in a puddle of tears.

Our life changed that day.

It was overwhelming and I really did not know how I was going to drive three hours. One of my best friends showed up at my door and said, "Pack your bag. I am driving you."

When we got to the hospital, I was met by the Chaplin, surgeon, police, sheriff, and a few others. We sat down and I was told that my husband did not make it through the surgery. They asked if I wanted to go see him one last time. My friend went with me and as I walked into the room to give him one more final kiss, I realized his spirit had already left. I kissed his cheek and left the hospital to our hotel room.

The next day we went to the hospital to collect my husband's belongings. We were met by the person in charge.

They asked me if there was anyone I wanted to see or talk to and I said, "I would like to see Roberta, my husband's nurse. I want to tell her thank you and tell her how much we both appreciated her and that she was a very special person to my husband and me."

As I walked down the long hallway and into her office, I was greeted with hugs from all of the staff. Roberta came and grabbed my hand and gently guided me behind closed doors. I was able to express our gratitude and love to her. What she did next was amazing. They did not perform an autopsy due to cause of death, but she pulled up some labs and began saying that what had been causing my husband pain was most likely the beginning of bone cancer.

She gave me peace that I would never have if I hadn't wanted to go thank her and express how grateful we were for her kindness. You see, if I hadn't thanked her or let her know how much we loved and appreciated her, then I wouldn't have known that this accident was an actual miracle. My husband left this earth at the top of his game. He didn't know what literally hit him from behind and he was saved from dying from a slow, painful death.

Sometimes we may not see what God's plan is, but trust that it the perfect plan for you!

KAREN HETRICK is the creator and owner of Heaven Scent Angel Sprays LLC. Karen is also certified angel card reader and Reiki Master. Her purpose on this earthly plane is helping others to connect with the angels and she has created Angel Sprays to assist with their experiences.

She teaches others that angels can feel, hear, and know us and that they are always supported by the heavenly realms. She will tell you that it is important to call upon the angels; they are legions just waiting to assist you in all the ways in your daily life.

Connect with Karen
Email: Heavenscentangelsprays@gmail.com
Facebook: Heaven Scent Angel Sprays LLC
Phone: 209-404-7960

Week 17

*Kindness is more important than wisdom, and
the recognition of this is the beginning of wisdom.*

~ Theodore Isaac Rubin

SOUL-SISTER

Decisions

"Be careful who you love," I was advised.

"Stay away from married men," I was ordered.

"Certainly, stay away from divorcés – far too much baggage," I was told.

But what happens when the years turn into decades and you haven't found your soulmate? Then your friends tell you to stay away from sad oldies who lived alone!

"You mean like me?" I would retort.

I was too busy and too social to feel a gap in my life, and I was out too much to ever feel lonely. But I could sense the purring of the cats that my friends intended to give me for my next birthday.

Then I met J.

I soon discovered that he came with three ready-made children from his first marriage.

"Run!" said a friend. "Run while you have the chance!"

But what do you do when you find someone who makes you feel like you have come home? What do you do when you find someone who makes you so happy and you know part of who he is, is *because* of his children and his past? Well, at fifty, when you have come to appreciate the fragility of life, and when you know what is important to you, such questions are easy to answer. We made a commitment to each other and got married. I then prayed that I would be able to understand emotionally as well as intellectually that his life didn't start the day I met him.

The Other Woman

She was dark and slim, fit and entrepreneurial. She could speak other languages and seemed confident and capable. She was his previous love. She was his first wife. And she was coming for Christmas!

She met me at the front door when I came home from work. She was wearing a smile and carrying two glasses and a bottle of bubbly.

"Cheers!" she said. "Let's talk!"

We found we had a lot in common. She had lived not far from where I had lived and we knew some of the same people. Our paths had almost crossed several times before. It was as if it were destiny that we were to eventually meet.

It's not always easy for either of us. Yet we are not children; we are adults. When you know you have made the right decision with your relationship then it's easier to appreciate the other requirements that are brought into the mix. A key consideration is whether you are prepared to support the other important people in your partner's life. This is not necessarily straightforward when there seems to be an expectation in our society that you won't like ex-wives and second wives. Yet, where does that leave the family unit especially when children are involved? Why should negativity win over the hope that there is a more congenial way?

Why should the way we approach a sister-in-law, or a brother-in-law be any different from the way we approach the mothers of the children of the men we love? Sometimes we do not have a choice as to who is in our lives, but we do have a choice about how we behave towards them. We can choose what thoughts and emotions we allow to surface and take space in our minds: distain and mistrust, or consideration and understanding.

Trying Our Best

It can be difficult to accommodate another woman into your home, whoever that might be, but especially if it is the ex-wife. Sometimes I have to dig deep when I am aware that I can never give my husband the firsts that she did. But it is not easy for her either. It is not helpful when society encourages the sentiment that it is the norm to dislike each other. Does this need to be? If there can be mutual respect, then surely, we all win? When there is a level of tolerance and kindness, then the children don't have to take sides; they don't need to miss out on valuable time with their parents, together or alone.

I hope divorce, especially when children are involved, doesn't always have to be a battlefield and full of stereotypical judgements. I am sure that with time we will see that we could have done things differently. But we made choices that we felt were appropriate with the understanding we had at the time. We tried to show kindness in a world where it is sometimes lacking.

His ex-wife will probably be around longer than our parents and some of our friends. So rather than engage in the all too easy ex-wife jokes, isn't it better to consider her a soul-sister with a shared mission to try to do the best for our extended family unit?

Living with Kindness

- ♥ I value the kindness and friendships my husband's family have given me.

- ♥ I am appreciative of the kindness my husband's ex-wife has shown me.

- ♥ I am grateful for the kindness her parents have also shown me. It means the world.

We have a choice as to whether we experience and demonstrate kindness on a moment-by-moment basis. It is easy to be kind to friends, but such a sentiment can also be offered to others. We offer kindness not necessarily because we resonate with those people, but because we recognise that they too are sentient beings worthy of such a grace.

Kindness by Choice

Offer kindness as you would a smile – the outward expression of your inner heart. To support this intention, I say a positive affirmation daily such as, *I am surrounded by kindness.* This helps to keep my vibration high and encourages me to notice and appreciate the kindness in my life and the opportunities I have to offer it to others.

In a world where you can choose - choose kindness.

TONIA BROWNE is a bestselling author, teacher, and coach. She is a strong advocate of inviting fun into our lives and encouraging people to see their world from a new perspective. Tonia's writing includes coaching strategies interspersed with spiritual insights and personal anecdotes. Tonia is a Heal Your Life® workshop leader and coach and was a primary-school assistant head.

Enjoy Tonia's books *Spiritual Seas* and also *Mermaids: An Empath and Introvert's Guide to Riding the Waves of Life.* Dive into her website and have fun with her beautiful mermaid cards and apparel, part of her "Diving into Life" series.

Connect with Tonia
Website: toniabrowne.com

Week 18

Kindness is the path that leads into your heart.
Kindness is also the path that leads out of your heart.

~ Diana Gogan

THE PATH INTO YOUR HEART

Our last walk through the house and outbuildings was eerily quiet. Echoes reverberated off the walls of the empty rooms. The stalls felt incomplete without the horses quietly munching on hay. The backyard seemed to be holding its breath in anticipation of the dogs bursting out of the house to chase some rabbit that had bravely entered their territory. I wanted to linger yet knew it was time to go.

I looked through the rearview mirror at Fire Horse Ranch, which was my home and business, as I sadly drove away for the last time. A part of my heart was aching, and it was difficult to see into the future with any clarity.

The emotions swirling within me left me feeling as if my life was precariously balanced on the edge of a rockslide. While the ground beneath me had temporarily stopped moving, I felt it could break loose again at any time.

The past few months had been shadowed with difficult personal situations. My marriage seemed to be hanging by a thread. Conversations with my husband left me with more questions than answers. *What did I want? Who was I now? What part had I played in bringing us to this point? Who did I want to be moving forward?* They were questions without any clear answers at that moment.

The challenges I was navigating in my marriage were only part of the story. We'd recently lost one of our beloved horses, and her presence was still deeply missed. For months I'd been planning an exciting new business venture. It suddenly fell apart. Because of that, a valued friendship hung in the balance. The house we were renting was suddenly put on the market and another suitable property couldn't be found. Stuck in the whirlwind, it felt as if my life was coming undone at the seams.

My spirit was tired. My soul encouraged me to reach out to trusted friends and mentors for support. Yet my pride and ego, afraid of what others might think, were adamant that I stay quiet and put on my "all is well" mask. And then there was this nagging thought I couldn't seem to shake. *I'm a spiritual life coach, one who others come to for guidance, and I can't seem to find my own way. What makes me think I'm qualified to help others?*

One day the murky haze lifted enough for me to realize that the story I was stuck in was one where I would never be the heroine. I was always the victim. The victim of circumstance, other people's actions, the economy, the weather, this thing and that thing. Living inside that story, I was focused on what I'd lost, trying to piece together a future that looked like the past.

Then it hit me.

If I recreated the past, I'd end up back in the same place I was currently in. I knew it was time to evolve by changing the story and my role within it.

With this new perspective, the rewrite began. Beliefs were challenged and changed. Attachments to habits, people, outcomes, familiarity, my comfort zone, and many other things were released. I began to recognize the new beginnings disguised as endings, and the unexpected surprises and opportunities that resulted.

One day a friend shared with me an audiobook she was enjoying, *29 Gifts: How a Month of Giving Can Change Your Life*. The title intrigued me since I was knee-deep inside my own change. I promptly downloaded and listened to the book. It was Cami Walker's personal story of her multiple sclerosis diagnosis and an unusual prescription she was given, which was to give one gift a day for twenty-nine days. I intently listened and began to wonder if this might also support me on my journey of reinvention.

I could imagine the fun and good feelings that random acts of kindness would elicit, but until then I had never really thought kindness to be a powerful part of transformation. It surprised me that my first gifts were to myself. Forgiveness, releasing judgment, a horseback ride, and a massage were some of those early gifts.

At first it felt awkward and self-centered. An analogy I've often heard about self-care helped me see it from a different perspective. The words of wisdom are these, "In the event of an emergency when flying on an airplane and the air masks drop, put yours on first before assisting others."

Taking care of my need for oxygen first allowed me to remain conscious and assist others.

I quickly recognized when I showed myself kindness, I wasn't as wrapped up in my own thoughts and needs because I was tending to those myself. It was then easier to see opportunities to offer kindness in the world around me.

I had another unexpected discovery. When I accepted kindness from myself, it then became easier to accept if from others. By openly receiving it, I inherently acknowledged that I was worthy and deserving of it.

From those first gifts to myself, I also came to understand that kindness is the path into my own heart. It helped clear limiting beliefs of worthiness. Now I could fully receive.

And that's where the magic happened. As kindness filled my heart, my desire to share with others grew. It wasn't that I wasn't kind before. What had changed was that I become more present to the bounty of opportunities around me.

I gave to a mother at the grocery store who was a few dollars short at checkout. I bought a cup of coffee for a stranger. I called a friend I hadn't spoken to in a long time to let her know I was thinking of her. I cleaned horse stalls for another friend before she got home from work. Each day I looked forward to seeing what opportunities presented themselves. Kindness became the path out of my heart because there was an abundance to share.

How was this life changing? I was no longer ruminating about my past. I was focused in the present. I was thinking about what I could do now and of the infinite opportunities that surrounded me. I was focused on the abundance that existed in my life. I thought about the beauty of the new home I was living in, the new possibilities in my business, and the many things I loved about my husband and our relationship.

Whatever you desire to change in your life or whatever sort of heroine you desire to be in your own story, kindness is a powerful part of your transformational journey. Harness its power! Kindness is the path into and out of your heart.

DIANA GOGAN a spiritual life coach and Wayfinder, spent years climbing the corporate ladder, yet at the same time become increasingly restless. She knew it was time to reconnect with the wisdom of her soul and the heartbeat of her spirit to discover the great work she is here to do. It is a journey she now expertly guides her clients on. Diana powerfully weaves together coaching, energy work, shamanic and nature practices, and equine-assisted coaching to create life changing experiences and opportunities for her clients. Visit her website to get her monthly insights, wisdom and resources to inspire you on your journey.

Connect with Diana
Website: DianaGogan.com

Week 19

To practice five things under all circumstances constitutes perfect virtue; these five are gravity, generosity of soul, sincerity, earnestness, and kindness.

~ Confucius

PLANTING A SEED OF KINDNESS

As the sun rises each morning, there is a hopefulness for the new day. Some people wake up excited and filled with joy, and others struggle to get out of bed, full of fear and anxiety of what this new day will bring. The first smile of the day is the beginning of kindness. If you start your day with a smile to yourself, you have already begun to plant the seed of kindness for your day.

A smile is probably one of the easiest ways to show kindness, not only for yourself but for anyone you encounter. This is especially true if you also make direct eye contact. You bring a connection of joy and kindness to everyone you greet this way, and I always believed that it's hard to be in a bad mood when you are smiling.

I truly think that using manners helps grow the kindness you are sharing. I say please and thank you when I am dealing with people. This includes strangers, such as a waitress or customer service rep. This make these people feel more comfortable, and the service they are doing for me always seems to be done with kindness. Showing them gratitude for the service they are giving me seems to also help them to show more kindness to others they are helping, and my garden of kindness continues to grow!

In February of 2019, I had one of those days when nothing was going right. I woke up with a bad cramp in my leg. I was hurting and frustrated. This seemed to be going on almost every day. As I stood up, the pain seemed to subside. It was there, but it was just not as severe. Looking into the mirror with my hair all over the place, I smiled and said, "Good morning, beautiful."

I started to giggle and then I was almost laughing. Even though I was not feeling well, the kindness to the woman in the mirror set my day for a more positive outlook.

Kindness has this effect on everyone. A smile, opening a door for a stranger, and even a compliment about how someone looks. Those acts will brighten the day of any person.

When someone won't make eye contact, I often say, "Wow, I love that color on you." This will usually make the person look up, and then I can smile and tell them to have a nice day. Not only do I usually get a smile back, but I feel good for sharing a kind word with someone that may have been having a lonely day!

As I became more comfortable with sharing kindness, I tried to would find ways that it would be unexpected, not only for a stranger, but for those in my life that sometimes I didn't think about. That was my family.

I realized that sometimes I was so complacent with my own family that I didn't even see that I was taking them for granted. I thought they had to know how I felt about them. Years ago as I sat at the table during a family function, I did not feel the type of happiness I would feel when I was sharing kindness to complete strangers, so I knew it was time for me to make a change and to make sure that my kindness always started with me and my family first.

As I focused on my family, I focused on the pleases and thank-yous that I talked about earlier. It definitely was noticed. I would see a little smile on my Mom's face each time I was courteous. With so much of our lives being on social media, I made sure to 'like' or 'love' posts from my family and made sure to comment on those same posts with genuine thoughtful comments.

Even though I am close with my family, we don't talk as much as I would like, so I try to send a text message that I am thinking about them and just checking in to see how they are doing. This kindness has changed our family and I now see it from everyone. Our family gatherings are even more enjoyable than they ever were before. Planting the kindness seed with my own family was one of the most enjoyable experiences for me. I challenged myself to make sure they knew that I was thinking about them and that I was grateful they were in my life!

Since I have embraced a life a gratitude and kindness, my whole life has changed. I feel and see the difference. One of my favorite acts of kindness is for strangers. I love to let people go in front of me at the grocery store, buy a coffee for the person behind me, help someone with loading their groceries into their car, and I always have bottled water and a Ziploc bag full of goodies in case I come across someone that is down on their luck.

One day I had given one of these bags to a man that was homeless and as I went back to my vehicle, I watched him go around the corner and share it with another couple. My kindness was shared to others that I didn't even see at first or I would have given each of them a bag. So I grabbed my last two bags, went back, and gave them to the man and thanked him for sharing. His tired smile stays with me to this day, and the gratitude I felt made me know that my kindness had made a difference. Sharing kindness is like planting a wonderful garden. It grows and so many others get joy from it!

HOLLY BIRD is an internationally bestselling author of the book *Shaken Dreams, A Journey from Wife to Caregiver*. She is a certified life coach and mentor with a focus on aging health-education and family.

She shares her wealth of life experiences, everything from spiritual and family mentoring, marriage, gardening, cooking, traveling, and her favorite being a grandma on her blog.

Connect with Holly
Website: Hollysbirdnest.com
Email: HollyBird@hollysbirdnest.com
Facebook: hollysbirdnest
Facebook: loveyourangels
Twitter: HOLLYJBIRD

Week 20

*The level of our success is limited only
by our imagination and no act of kindness,
however small, is ever wasted.*

~ Aesop

FOR THE LOVE OF PUDGIE-BOO

Whatever happened to kindness and goodwill to all? Crowded stores filled with stressed-out, grumpy shoppers trying to get the best deals, or grabbing the most sought-after toy before the store sells out.

They push and shove each other out of the way to reach the rare item they have been searching for. It seems like Black Friday brings out the worst in people, maybe that is the real meaning behind the name.

If only there was a way to show people that happiness is not what is in their shopping carts, and that love is not measured by how much they spend. After all, shouldn't there be as much joy in giving a heart-felt gift as receiving one? Where is the love? Where is the kindness?

Personally, I prefer giving gifts that are not store-bought. A homemade gift is something made with love, whether it is an item, a service, or a simple card. No matter what it is; it took time and energy to plan and create and is usually more personal, since it was created just for that person. I always appreciate those types of gifts and have tried to pass that value onto my girls.

From a very young age, my girls would spend weeks trying to find or design the perfect gifts to give that weren't purchased in stores. It could be a craft item like stuffed animals they made out of socks, tailored to what each recipient liked most. Sometimes they gave something they made in school, or they even found a treasure around the house and wrapped it up in special packaging. It was always a big secret that they thought up and initiated all on their own, without any help from us grownups. And I never knew what we would find when the box was opened.

One of my favorite memories was when Kiara was seven and Mackenzie was four. Mackenzie had a little stuffed animal that she took everywhere she went. It was her constant companion for years, a small yellow duck, about three inches tall, that she had lovingly named Pudgie-Boo. Nobody really knows how she came up with the name, but he did have a pudgy belly and a tuft of scruffy fluff atop his head.

He was small enough for her to put in her pocket and take with her everywhere. Pudgie-Boo even slept on her pillow. He was well worn, a little dirty, and without a doubt, he was well loved.

Christmas was approaching, and I noticed Mackenzie sneaking into her room with a box and some wrapping paper. She banned me from coming anywhere near her room, saying it was "top secret." She emerged a short time later carrying a box clumsily wrapped in purple tissue with a bow perched on top, and a tag that read, "To Kiara."

She was beaming from ear to ear as she held the box, bouncing up and down, bursting with excitement. "Can we open presents now?"

"No. We need to wait until Christmas. It's only a couple weeks away," I replied, even though I was dying to find out what was in the box.

She asked this almost every day, not at all interested in the packages with her name on them. She just couldn't wait to give her sister the special gift.

The day finally arrived when we would exchange gifts between the four of us. Our tradition is that everyone chooses one gift to open at home on Christmas Eve, and then we take the rest to the larger family gathering.

Mackenzie jumped up to retrieve the purple package from under the tree. "Kiara has to open this one!" She handed it to her sister and sat right in front of her, almost trembling with excitement. "Now, open it now! Open it, open it!"

Kiara obliged and began tearing open the package. The paper fell to the floor and the box opened. She carefully pulled away the layers of tissue paper to find her surprise. Inside the box was none other than Pudgie-Boo, her sister's favorite toy and most prized possession.

Tears filled my eyes. I was deeply moved by Mackenzie's kind gesture, but I was also confused. Why would she give away her favorite toy? And why was she so excited about it?

After we finished with all the other gifts, I pulled Mackenzie aside and asked her about the gift. "Why would you give Pudgie-Boo to your sister?"

She looked at me with so much joy and love in her eyes and said, "Because I love it and I knew it would make her happy."

I was dumbfounded. I didn't know what to do. My first reaction was to say, "No you can't give that away!" But I didn't want to take away from her excitement and joy. Despite my bewilderment, a bigger realization hit me. Here I was stressing out about so many things that didn't really matter, and my four-year-old came along and showed me what was really important.

She gave her love in a way that was most impactful. She gave from her heart without giving it a second thought. Beyond that, she didn't feel sad about parting with her beloved Pudgie-Boo, but was bursting with joy and excitement to give that gift of love to the person that meant the most to her. Why? Because it would make her sister happy.

Kiara graciously accepted the gift but knowing how much Pudgie-Boo meant to her little sister, she told Mackenzie that she would be happier if Pudgie-Boo stayed with her because Pudgie-Boo loved her so much. They both gave lovingly from their hearts and felt only joy in giving. Still to this day, they are both more excited to give a gift to someone than they are to receive one themselves.

I continue to be blown away by the kindness of these girls and by the lessons they have taught me, when I thought I was teaching them. They have shown me how even the smallest acts of kindness and love can convey a powerful message. You don't need to be rich to give from the heart or to find ways to show kindness and love to others. The shortest path to joy is finding ways to make another smile. And finally, they showed me that a gift of love is no sacrifice, but a joy passed from one to another.

KRIS GROTH is a spiritual mentor, energy healer, bestselling author of *Soul-iloquy: A Novel of Healing, Soul Connection & Passion, Soul-iloquy Companion Journal: A Conversation With Your Soul*, and co-author of four other bestselling books.

She is passionate about helping people connect more deeply to their own truth to promote healing and restore balance to the body, mind, heart, and soul. Kris serves clients around the world through her healing and spiritual mentoring sessions, online courses, and powerful guided sound healing meditations using crystal singing bowls. Visit her website to claim your "Sacred Sound Healing Meditation & Affirmation Gift Set."

Connect with Kris
Website: KrisGroth.com
Email: krisgroth.unlimited@gmail.com
Facebook: bodywhisperstherapy
Twitter: kris_groth

Week 21

*True beauty is born through our actions and
aspirations and in the kindness we offer to others.*

~ Alek Wek

KINDNESS 2.0 – THE NEXT GEN OF KINDNESS CRUSADERS

Kindness (noun): the quality of being friendly, generous, and considerate; a kind act.

— English Oxford Living Dictionaries

One of my goals as a Kindness Crusader is to empower my kids. This generation of children is growing up with cellphones in their hands at a very early age, countless hours of streaming, and exposure to intense anger, insecurities, and hate on social media. This is frightening and sometimes difficult for parents to navigate. We are the first generation of parents who have had to raise children alongside technology and social media. We are all becoming more disconnected, segregated, materialistic, and stressed out. Yes, even five-year-olds are stressed out these days. Bullying behavior is rampant in workplaces and schools. I could go on and on about electronics and social media; it's a love-hate relationship for me, but that's a whole other book. Instead, I choose to focus my parenting through kindness and gratitude.

What if kindness and compassion became the focus in our daily lives?

Could we change the world for our kids for the better?

Empowering kids is the first step to building a stronger community. I believe that if we live our lives – and teach our children to live their lives – centered around kindness, compassion, and gratitude, then we can change the world. After all, kindness is contagious!

I recall the first time someone in front of me paid for my order in the drive-thru. My kids were with me and when we got to the window and the girl said that the driver ahead of us paid for our order, my kids were amazed. As we drove away, we started a conversation about random acts of kindness. Before we got to our destination, my kids were brainstorming all the different ways they could give something to others in this random way. That day they felt the power of kindness and instantly wanted to return that feeling to someone else.

Research has shown that devoting resources to others, rather than having more and more for yourself, brings about lasting wellbeing. Can you recall a time someone was kind to you? How did that feel? I imagine it felt pretty good for you. Now, turn that around. Can you remember a time that you were kind to another person? Do you remember how you felt? I imagine you had similar feelings to what you felt when someone was kind to you. Kindness affects both the giver and the receiver. Kindness is a win-win.

"Kindness is a language which the deaf can hear and the blind can see."—Mark Twain

Kindness is not something that demands a lot from you. Simply put, kindness is doing no harm to others. It's about losing your judgments, biting your tongue, and dropping the need to be right all the time. It's about flipping it around and asking yourself how you would feel if someone did this to you? If you wouldn't like it, then don't do it to others.

Raising a Kindness Crusader

I'll never forget the day my son came home from school and asked me to post on Facebook asking my friends to donate their old coats to him because he was doing his own coat drive for the homeless. He said that he already stood up in front of his class at school and made a plea for them to bring their unwanted coats to school the next day. He then rallied his hockey teammates to bring their unused coats. In the end, he dropped off seventy-five coats, snow pants, toques, mitts, and socks to the homeless shelter that winter. It was amazing! I had nothing to do with any of this; it was completely driven by him. When I heard the title of this book the first person, I thought of was my son. He is definitely a kindness crusader. He also happens to be an author in this book, too. It is truly an honor to be his mom.

A Rally Cry for Kindness

We need more kindness in the world, in our homes, in our communities, at our workplaces, and online. And it starts with us. With you. And me. It's not good enough to just talk about it, we need to be a positive force for change and take action!

We become kinder with practice.

No act of kindness is ever wasted. So, go ahead and start practicing! Start by doing one small thing every day for someone. Incorporate the smallest acts of kindness into your everyday life and notice the ripple effects. Open your eyes, heart, and mind to the ways that you can inject kindness into your day.

- ♥ Can you help someone?

- ♥ Can you bite your tongue and be empathetic to the situation?

- ♥ Can you be kind to yourself?

- ♥ How can you spread positive vibes?

- ♥ How can you teach others to be kind?

- ♥ How can you pay it forward?

- ♥ Can you start or get involved in a kindness project?

"Be kind whenever possible. It is always possible." — *Dalai Lama*

We have included a kindness calendar in this book that may give you some daily inspiration. In my family, we are going to make a game using the kindness calendar to see how many acts of kindness we can do in our day, week or month.

1. Print the monthly calendar and post it somewhere you'll be sure to see it every day.

2. Make time for each day's challenge. If you need to swap days or complete multiple tasks on the weekend, that's okay.

3. Make time to reflect as a family. This is an important step and teachable moment for raising the next generation of kindness crusaders.

There are countless online resources and organizations whose entire mission is to spread kindness. Jump on the kindness crusade and get involved.

Be the reason someone smiles today.

Kindness is free -- sprinkle that stuff everywhere!

Kindness -- a simple way to tell another struggling soul that there is still love to be found in this world.

Be kind.

NIKKI GRIFFIN is a certified autism travel professional and cruise specialist who owns her own travel agency in Calgary, Canada. She married the love of her life and finds joy every day with her hilarious daughter and witty son who is also an author in this book.

Nikki has written two bestselling books on gratitude and happiness, and enjoys writing blog posts, newsletters, and social media content for other small business owners. Her passion is helping others succeed.

Boost your brilliant self, engage your sense of adventure, and enjoy a more fulfilled life!

Connect with Nikki
Email: nikki3griffin@gmail.com

Week 22

Love and kindness are never wasted. They always make a difference. They bless the one who receives them, and they bless you, the giver.

~ Barbara De Angelis

KINDNESS BEGINS WITHIN

From early on, we're taught certain core concepts about how to be a good human. With the trials and tribulations of life, the ups and downs, the good days and the bad days, we struggle to keep these concepts at the forefront of our minds. We go about our days and hope that we can do better, be better, and live better lives. Yet, in the thick of things, when chaos runs rampant and triggers have all been sprung, we forget. We set aside our hearts, our teachings, our traditions, and go with the flow. We keep looking back over our shoulders remembering, trying to stop the inevitable drive to move forward and succeed, and losing ourselves along the way.

We become a shell of our former selves. That self is the spirited inner child, the believer of dreams where all is possible. Instead we become that being we no longer recognize in the mirror. We move in automation about our days, speaking, working, doing our daily duties, but the spark is gone. We start to tear ourselves down, flustered with how we handle ordinary tasks. We can become cruel or heartless. We can become hateful or impatient, rude to others or our own selves. Instead of seeing the positive, we begin to only see the negative and are no longer able to discern those qualities that made us feel worthy. Mostly, in the passing of time, we've become unkind. We become unkind to the world, but that isn't the saddest part; we become unkind to ourselves.

Once the unkind words begin, they start to flow, bubbling forth like molten lava, scarring everything in their paths. The simple act of being unkind has ramifications that ripple outwards, changing us and our perceptions of life itself. We become battered and bruised. Our self-worth takes a nosedive of massive proportions and soon all becomes trivial, senseless, and pointless.

Are we irredeemable? Have we gone so far that we can't find our way back? These are questions we ask ourselves and in the asking, we find the answers. We as human beings, energetic beings of light and compassion, have this remarkable ability for change. For in all things, it begins within. Looking deep within ourselves, seeing all the darkness that has spread like a cancer across our spirits, we can begin the arduous task of repairing that which has been damaged. By using simple sentences and words, we can show ourselves kindness. You thought I was going to say something else, didn't you?

In the Random House dictionary, the meaning for kindness is "the state or quality of being kind." I wish to share kindness with all creatures and beings, but first I realized I had to give this to myself. I needed to stop knocking myself down, calling myself hateful names, and seeing myself as inferior to everything and everyone else. By becoming tolerant, tender, and gentle in the treatment of my own mind, body, and spirit, I could then share the gift of kindness to the world at large. If I could show myself a little affection, grace, and courtesy, then I would gain a greater capacity to be a healer instead of a destroyer.

Each day, I carve away at the bitterness that resides within and I heal. Each day, I take one step forward, pushing towards the goal of accepting the imperfect person I am. I smile more at everyone who crosses my path, letting them see the real me. I speak to myself in soft tones and when I feel anger rise at a mistake I've made, I stop and breathe. I give myself the right to stumble and when it happens, I delicately dust myself off and keep going. This is the mission I've set forth for myself, the battle I will wage as I live the rest of my days. For no longer will I belittle myself, criticizing every action I take, and judging all that I do. I choose to be a crusader of kindness and by healing the wounds within me, may I be blessed to heal the wounds of others.

ROCHELLE ENGLISH lives in Texas with her dashing Brit of a husband and their snarky princess. Because of her love of books, she's been a voracious reader all her life. A Jill of all trades, she has a wide range of skills and jobs in her repertoire but has decided to pursue her dream of becoming a freelance writer and indie author with a dash of photography on the side. When she's not contemplating stories, she can be found enjoying every moment with her family. The three of them are inseparable.

Connect with Rochelle
Website: writerrmenglish.wixsite.com/home
Email: writerrmenglish@gmail.com
Instagram: r.m.english
Facebook: WriterR.M.English

Week 23

*It's not our job to play judge and jury, to determine
who is worthy of our kindness and who is not. We just
need to be kind, unconditionally and without ulterior motive,
even - or rather, especially - when we'd prefer not to be.*

~ Josh Radnor

HELLO KINDNESS!

How does one measure kindness? Is it in hugs, sweet gestures, or love notes? I have always equated kindness to something magical because kindness honors another person's feelings, worth, story, wellbeing, and happiness. It holds a higher intention to bring validation, aid, and comfort to another human soul as a way to elevate spirit or heal someone's condition.

My study of spirituality and compassion has made me quite curious about the nature of kindness. If everybody has the capacity to express this goodness, then why does there seem to be a shortage of tolerance, warmth, empathy, and inclusion in the world? Could it be that society is conditioning us to ration our love?

I am a "possibilitarian." That means that I believe that kindness is necessary to my own survival. While I don't look to convert you, I would ask you to re-evaluate all preconceived ideas that you may have about the value of good deeds and humanity. In my humble opinion, love validates our existence. Therefore, we really can change the world through noble gestures of kindness.

What are you currently doing to raise the vibration of love in your community?

Should you have difficulty answering that question then I would challenge you to think about unique ways that you can share your gifts and passion with your family, friends, neighbors, employees, customers, and local organizations. It may be through art, music, writing, or volunteering.

There are infinite ways to express kindness. When we bring forward our joy and plug it into some form of service in the world, that's when we'll experience another level of connection, personal fulfillment, and higher consciousness. It allows us to get in touch with our divine self.

Contrary to popular belief, money, fame, power, or social popularity don't improve our relationships or guarantee happiness. Kindness can actually heal social problems and mend the broken spirit of millions of human beings across the world.

For those who still believe that we must take political sides, bully those who disagree with us, reject those who look and pray differently, or who love outside the traditional norms of society, you may need some deeper reflection on "heartisty." Now, what is that?

Heartistry is the highest expression of the soul. It's where heart, service, and spirituality align together to bring forward the highest good for all human beings. All gestures are intended to elevate people and increase the positive flow of energy. You see, kindness does not operate with any agenda or seek anything in return; it's wholesome by nature.

Now, I'm sure that you have been the recipient of another person's thoughtfulness. Perhaps a kind soul bought your coffee in the line at Starbucks. Maybe you found a mason jar of flowers on your porch from a kind neighbor, or maybe some beautiful stranger paid for your bridge toll. Well, today I'm challenging you to look deeper at kindness. Why does kindness matter more than ever, and why it is important to your psyche?

When people show us kindness, it's like hitting the "like" button in our brain. There's a physiological response that happens. Endorphins, dopamine, serotonin, and oxytocin are released. These natural chemicals and hormones reduce pain and stimulate positive feelings. Here is some fantastic news. The response in our bodies is the same whether we are the recipient or the giver. You see, kindness will promote a higher state of joy and wellbeing. Therefore, when it comes to kindness, the soul has nothing to lose and everything to gain.

I used to sit in church as a little girl listening to scripture and sermons and wonder what exactly the universe had in store for my life. I now know that the intention for my life is no different than yours or my neighbor's. It doesn't matter what social class we are from, where we grow up, or what kind of family dynamic we've had. Each life story will include some tale of kindness.

In the larger scheme of life, we are all called to serve something greater than ourselves, and we have the ability to reach everyone if we choose to band together in our kindness. You see, it's not about one person saving the world. *It's imperative that we ALL do our small part.*

Some may refer to kindness as generosity, humanity, service, charity, or compassion. It really makes no difference what name you use. What matters is only that you secure some higher practice in your life. We are here to love, and love gives every single human being a sense of purpose while they are here on this earth.

Brave acts of kindness and affection allow us to evolve in our human experience, transcend obstacles, and empower the next generation. We are invited to exchange kindness, conversation, and affection with people from all walks of life. From loved ones to strangers, there's no telling how our warm energy can change the spirit of another human being. At least there's no telling until we are actually brave enough to do something selfless and kind.

The truth is that when kindness is motivated by the intention to do something good, another level of social and spiritual consciousness arrives in the world. It gives us a better understanding of ourselves and how vulnerability and imperfection can bring us all together. Did you know that showing up for others in times of grief and difficulty will actually heal yourself just as much as it helps the person that you are helping?

The power of kindness can't be overstated. We don't need a reason to express kindness. "Just because" remains the most profound explanation for love. Every time you turn on the news ask yourself if love could have made the difference. Compassion, humanity, and inclusion are the only things that will actually improve society and heal the soul of the world.

Now, while I'm standing on my soap box, I want to remind you of one very important point. Kindness begins with some higher appreciation for your own value and worth. We simply cannot give what we do not have. Therefore, self-care and thoughtful deeds must begin with ourselves.

When I think about a true warrior on this subject, I always come back to Mother Teresa. She reminds us that there is no deed too small. Every act of kindness met with some intention to love, heal, comfort, and bring forth joy has the power to elevate the vibration that we all draw energy from.

Kindness gives every human being a sense of purpose. While it's immeasurable, we do know one magical truth. The more love we give, the more love we have. It is the only currency that actually matters.

It's true that we sometimes forget that the air we collectively breathe exists because of the kindness of the universe. We are here on purpose, and the quality of our lives is based on some larger dedication to improve society one deed at a time.

In a world where we can be just about anything, Kindness *does* matter! It doesn't have to be extravagant, just heartfelt. Be good, my friends. Allow your soul to shine through gentle acts of kindness. There is nothing simpler and more extraordinary.

With Kindness and Gratitude,

Krista Gawronski

KRISTA GAWRONSKI is a philanthropist and the bestselling spiritual author of *Soul Purpose* and *Be Good*. She is a mind, body, and medicine practitioner. Over the last twenty-five years she has been designing a lifestyle around kindness and philanthropy. She is passionate about blogging and speaking to people about compassion and humanity. She refers to this higher consciousness as "*heartistry*." Krista resides in Sonoma County and has created a soulful group that meets monthly to talk about life called "Dare to Shine." For more information about her work and books please consult her webpage.

Connect with Krista
Website: KristaGawronski.com

Week 24

There are realities we all share, regardless of our nationality, language, or individual tastes. As we need food, so do we need emotional nourishment: love, kindness, appreciation, and support from others.

~ J. Donald Walters

CREATE EACH DAY FROM YOUR HEART,
IT WILL NEVER LEAD YOU ASTRAY …

Kindness is in my DNA.

My mom was disabled but taught us girls about being kind since others had it, as she said, "a hell of a lot worse." She never complained of pain on prescription medications as a quick fix.

I was thankful to be a part of 4-H club from ages nine to nineteen. As I grew into an adult, I continued my journey of kindness, citizenship, joy, and love.

About six years ago, I took interest in a spiritual community that promoted inner growth and self-care, which resulted in me living a life of bliss. During this time, I would communicate to Roxy, the administer of this community. I had taken my first yoga class with her at a Sedona retreat in September. Roxy had always been the first one on the line to chat with regarding the classes, concerns, and setting up payments.

At the time, her hip was causing her some discomfort.

Early December 2017, my mentor came online to announce that Roxy was taken to the hospital with a dislocated hip. My mentor was crying while she announced this. As I sat looking at my screen, tears rolled down my cheeks. My hand went to my heart.

Roxy always said, "Hand on your heart."

A little bit later, it was announced that Roxy had breast cancer that metastasized.

I heard loud and clear, *you must do something now …*

On December 11. 2017, I reached out to my mentor mentioning a fundraiser with painted rocks for Rockin' Roxy. I could personalize anything. We could possibly have a twenty-four-hour Rockin' Roxy-

A-Thon? My mentor loved the idea. She suggested five different designs to choose from and with that I started painting.

Angels, peace, miracles, love and Rockin' Roxy were painted on each of five rocks and sent to Arizona for review. During this time, I went out of my comfort zone and asked two rock groups in Petaluma to donate rocks for this event. I offered a card reading to each person as they bought their painted rocks. Each person had a story to share about their own journey with disease. I was honored to listen to them all. Even though the rocks were for Roxy's fundraiser, I felt that they were doing so much more and *meant* so much more.

I personally painted two hundred rocks. The total was three hundred painted rocks. Each rock was wrapped in bubble wrap. There were three boxes totaling eighty pounds and mailed to Arizona on February 26, 2018. There was going to be a fundraiser on March 3, 2018 and the rocks were in transit. The rocks bought in over $1500 and my heart was filled with so much joy. I painted forty-four more, and additional twenty-three pounds and shipped them to Arizona as my mentor was doing an online fundraiser too. On March 17, 2018, I was hired to do a rock painting at a friend's home for St. Patrick's Day, entertaining children. I explained Roxy's journey. We painted from 11 am to 4 pm. At the end, each child came up to me with a painted rock for Roxy saying, "I hope your friend gets better, please give her this rock."

A donation was made and sent to Roxy. We also sent her photos, a card, and rocks from the children. The donations provided funding for alternative treatments that were not supported by western medicine.

Roxy is rocking a miracle! Her healing journey of love, support, possibility, laughter, hope, and miracles continued. On April 10, 2019, she celebrated her fifty-eight birthday and continues to be a teacher to many as her healthy journey continues more strongly than ever.

This experience taught me that when you get a message from spirit to do something, don't think; do it. I had the ability to paint rocks; I didn't think about any costs whatsoever. I reached out with an idea. My mentor and her team created the space to bring in the revenue that Roxy needed. I asked for extra rocks to accomplish my vision and a hundred arrived. All of that was totally out of my comfort zone.

Today, Roxy continues to teach all of us amazing healing techniques with her journey of wellness. She is consistently committed to being healthy. I'm beyond grateful for this experience and would do it all over again! As Roxy always says. "Hand on your heart. Create each day from your heart. It will never lead you astray."

VICKI ANN MARTINELLI is an authentic, no-bullshit life coach, a successful insurance broker by day and an authentic Reiki Master, mind-body-spirit practitioner, certified angel intuitive card reader, spiritual teacher and ordained minister by night.

She brings her boundless energy and infectious motivational style to all her workshops and readings, helping others recognize their blessings in the midst of blame. She is CEO (cheerful energy operator) of Kindness Matters Project in her 55+ community where they create monthly acts of kindness. *Spread the glitter, bye-bye bitter!* To contact Vicki or learn more about her work, email her.

Connect with Vicki
Email: ladyvicki@hotmail.com
Join a kindness rock group in your area.

Week 25

I simply do not think that yelling, swearing, threatening or belittling will get you to the place you want to be faster than kindness, understanding, patience and a little willingness to compromise.

~ Rachel Nichols

KINDNESS TURNS THE DARKNESS TO LIGHT

Our big family reunion in San Francisco was supposed to be an event filled with light, love, and laughter. All our matriarchs had gathered on stage and were treating us to a concert of folklore songs. My mother was right there among them and as I watched her, my heart broke into pieces.

For the previous nine months, my mother had been in excruciating leg pain. She struggled just to walk. Dozens of trips to different doctors failed to yield a diagnosis or a treatment to alleviate her symptoms.

While she'd willed herself to attend this family reunion and perform for us all, I could see the hurt and despair in her eyes. Worse yet, I knew her time was limited. I had a horrible foreboding about her that occurred even before she felt her first pangs of pain nine months earlier.

The confirmation of my worries came a few months after the concert. I sat in the doctor's office with Mom as he finally gave us the news that would change the trajectory of so many lives.

Mom had a rare form of uterine cancer that had progressed to its final stages, spreading to many other parts of her body. Honestly, I don't even remember what they told us about how much time she had left. Numb, deflated, and exhausted, I could only imagine how *she* was feeling.

After being diagnosed, Mom started chemotherapy. It was at this time that I came to understand that both Mom and myself shared a character trait; we preferred to do things all on our own! After her cancer diagnosis, we both had to put away our pride and be open to receive the love and support offered to us for the long, rough journey ahead.

Reflecting back now, it must have been difficult for Mom to do this. She was a person who was all about giving not taking. She was always very generous with her words and time and to this day, I still run into people who tell me how much they miss her, or delight in showing me jewelry she gave them. There's no doubt she sprinkled kindness wherever she went.

But Mom's cancer forced her to be open to receiving. She received the same love and kindness from those around her that she'd always shown to them. And boy, did she get a lot! Over the next fourteen months, our entire family received an immense amount of love and support from so many people.

My father also displayed an immense capacity for change. Usually a tough and proud man, he softened to care for Mom. It was so beautiful to walk into their home and see him standing at the stove making her lunch. Even though Mom could have managed it herself, she knew he wanted to help her, and she gracefully allowed him that gift.

What surprised me the most during those days was Mom's ability to push on. Even on her toughest days, she still got up and dressed in nice clothes, put on her stylish wig to cover her hair loss, dabbed on her red lipstick and went out to enjoy herself. Finally, after all years of doing for others, she was doing for herself.

Our friends, family, and greater community banded together to help Mom enjoy herself. They took her out to lunch and on shopping expeditions. They spent hours on the phone with her and visited her often, showering her with so much love just as she'd done for them. I still pull out the pictures of the memories they created during this time and I smile as I remember.

Throughout all of this, Mom always strove to put on a courageous face. She continued laughing and cracking her racy jokes to make others comfortable, hoping to distract them from the reality ahead. Even during her darkest times, she wanted to be a light for others. She continued to show up decked out like a movie star with a million-dollar smile and she'd do this even while dragging her oxygen tank around so she could breathe.

October 17, 2002 was Mom's fiftieth birthday. Just like she had always surprised us with fancy gifts and delicious meals on our special days, we did the same for her. We told her to get dressed up in her best outfit as Dad was taking her out. But instead, my godmother and godfather arrived in a limousine to sweep her off to a fancy dinner in the city. She was so excited!

The surprise didn't end there. When they arrived at the restaurant, my siblings, god brothers and god sister were there waiting. It was an amazing night and Mom radiated light. I still have the picture of that day and it's impossible to tell she was sick and only two months away from transitioning from the physical world to meet her creator.

Two months later, I was seven-months pregnant and it was Christmas. With a sense of worry in my stomach, I sat back and watched the evening unfold. Mom sat on the couch with her oxygen tank and did her best to remain hopeful, knowing full well the end was near.

When I arrived at my parents' house on January 8, 2003, Mom was sleeping peacefully. The hospice nurse compassionately told us her time was near, and I remember being so grateful to her for her kindness through that very scary time.

Word that Mom was starting to make her transition spread quickly to our family, friends, and greater community. Within a few short hours, my parents' home was filled with loved ones. Several of our priests also came to support us.

As we waited for our matriarch to take her last breath, it was difficult to express emotions we felt. She was leaving us forever and she was still so young. We didn't have enough time with her; we still needed her for so many more weddings, births, baptisms, birthdays. But it was God's will and there was nothing we could do.

On the night of January 10, 2003, Mom took her last breath. She looked so beautiful and peaceful. In a moment that was supposed to be the most horrible of my life, I can now see it as one of the most beautiful.

Mom was at home surrounded by the tremendous love of her family and friends. All Mom had shown everyone for so many years was being returned, showering down upon us. While nothing could take away our pain, we could still see that the love and support from our friends, family, and community was a precious gift.

This gift of kindness is something we all have within us. Yes, life can be hectic and challenging, but it's important to remember all humans experience the same things. The touch of your kindness can make all the difference to someone in pain. It's a power you hold, so when it comes time, will *you* show your strength and offer kindness?

GRACE REDMAN owns and manages one of the most successful employment agencies in the San Francisco Bay Area for the past twenty years. She is also a success coach who helps guide others to diminish their negative mental chatter and create the lives they have been dreaming of.

If you are interested in learning more about Grace and to see how she can guide you to diminish your own negative mental chatter and create a life you love, please visit her website or email her.

Connect with Grace
Website: daretoachieve.com
Email: grace@daretoachieve.com

Week 26

Three things in human life are important.
The first is to be kind. The second is to
be kind. And the third is to be kind.

~ Henry James

THE KINDNESS PROJECT

What is the Kindness Project? Before we get into that, I think that we should start by asking what is kindness? Kindness is doing something for a person that makes them feel happy, appreciated, and valued. The dictionary describes kindness as the quality of being friendly, generous, and considerate. Kindness is all the different ways — big and small — that we express care, concern, and consideration for ourselves and those we share this world with.

If somebody is having a really bad day and they drop their books in the hallway at school, then that would probably make them feel pretty unhappy, right? If you see that they are a bit angry or flustered, then you should stop and help them pick up their books because that would probably make them feel better. There are opportunities to be kind in every situation. Sometimes the ways are obvious and sometimes you have to look a little harder, but you always have the chance to be kind no matter where you are or what you're doing.

Why should you be kind?

- ♥ You make people feel good.

- ♥ You feel good and are less stressed.

- ♥ People will do kind things for you in the future.

- ♥ Kindness makes the world a better place.

- ♥ You build a reputation of being "the kind guy."

- ♥ People may need a little kindness in their life.

- ♥ People appreciate kindness.

- ♥ It's quick and easy to do.

- ♥ Everyone can do it – even little kids.

When I am at school or out in public, I try to make sure that I am always doing the kind thing. When I see someone wearing merchandise of my favorite sports team, then I'll say, "good team." When we go out shopping, I always make sure to thank the cashier when we buy something. When I leave school, I always make sure to say "goodnight" to the teacher or tell him or her to have a good evening. That teacher may have had a really bad day and saying something like that could make him or her feel valued and happy. Plus, it makes me feel good and puts a smile on my face too.

Parents have a thankless job and they do so many things for so many people and most of the time they go without thanks. They put roofs over our heads and food on our tables. They provide us with water, clothes, heat, air conditioning, love, and happiness. They do the most epic things for us! If your parents are still alive, then I want you to put down this book and call them or go over to them and give them a big giant hug and say thank you. Imagine how they will feel after you acknowledge them and say thanks?

Siblings also deserve kindness. Siblings can become pretty competitive with each other, fighting over things, fighting about who did it better, or fighting for Mom and Dad's attention. But they can also develop greatness in one another, too. They look out for us. They help us with our homework, and they make life pretty fun.

Our pets deserve kindness as well. They play with us. They cuddle with us, enjoy life with us, and they give us something to do. When I see people being unkind to animals, it breaks my heart. My mom always says that a true judge of character is how someone treats animals and his or her server at a restaurant. No matter how educated, rich, or cool you believe you are, how you treat people and animals ultimately tells all.

Last but most certainly not least, there are strangers. They could be your teacher, your doctor or lawyer, your milkman, your caretaker, the man at the bakery, the woman driving the bus, or the guy cleaning the windows, but what they all have in common is that they all deserve kindness.

The Kindness Project

Now, the moment you've all been waiting for – the Kindness Project. It's not actually as hard as you might think. All it involves is one single rule. Just like everything in life, it has rules. The only rule for the Kindness Project is that you must have fun! My philosophy in life is that if you are not having fun then you are doing life wrong. This is true for me at least.

Okay, back to the Kindness Project.

Your goal for a whole year is to do as many random acts of kindness as you can that will simply get people to say, " thank you." That's not as hard as you thought it was going to be, right? We have even included a kindness calendar in this book that will make it so easy for you to do something kind every day. Now, get out there and spread some kindness!

Different ways that we can be kind

- ♥ We can start by saying "good morning", "good afternoon", and "good evening" to the people we love and the people that we don't even know.

- ♥ Smiling at someone or just saying "hi."

- ♥ Say "please" and "thank you" when somebody does something nice for you.

- ♥ Holding the door for someone is a great way to show respect and kindness. It is important to respect everyone even if they have wronged you in the past. They have done good things too.

- ♥ Compliments are a great way to show someone that they have a rockin' style. "Hey Mom, I like your shirt." "Yo Derek, where did you get those shorts?" "How many times do I have to tell you, those shoes look so good on you!" You may not like something about someone. Instead, you could compliment the dinner they made you, or the shoes they wore to work, but make sure not to be negative about what you don't like about that person. How would you feel if someone came up to you and said, "Dude, those shoes suck?"

- ♥ You can also say "bless you" to someone when they sneeze, or cough.

- ♥ Be kind online. Don't bully people or write mean things. Instead, encourage and support others. Be an online kindness crusader!

The most important thing in today's day and age with all its violence, hate, mistrust, and rudeness is that we all have to remember to be kind. Be kind to your mom, dad, siblings, friends, neighbors, mailman, milkman, store clerk, teacher, and boss. Anyone that you could ever imagine, be kind to them.

Please.

LANDEN BALLENDINE is a 14-year-old, grade-nine student who likes to spend time playing video games, hanging out with friends, playing baseball, basketball, and hockey. He strives for good grades, good friends, a job as a personal trainer, and wants to spend three weeks traveling all around Europe. He believes that once everyone is kind to each other there will truly be world peace.

Week 27

I've been searching for ways to heal myself,

and I've found that kindness is the best way.

~ Lady Gaga

YES, YOU MATTER

Your random acts of kindness, friendly hellos, positive words, gestures, and smiles matter more than you may ever know.

I experienced a very harsh world growing up and when I was thirteen, I attempted suicide. Many decades later suicide had become a silent epidemic and I knew I needed to do more. I have learned from my own experience that no matter how hard and unfair life may seem, the struggle is worth the victory.

As I thought back to what helped me continue to choose life during the darkest and loneliest times of my life, I could often trace it back to the kindness and words of others who had no idea what I was going through.

To be noticed and treated with kindness was like a rush of warmth. It was like a brilliant light that penetrated the darkness clouding my soul. To the person being kind, it may have seemed like just a little thing but to me their kind act was a ray of hope.

Because of this, it has been a personal mission of mine to always notice others and be kind.

About a year ago, I started to hand out You Matter bags everywhere I go. I wanted to be that person for someone else. My bags include a handwritten note, a "You Matter" lip balm, and sometimes candy or other fun things.

The experiences of handing out the bags have been priceless. Sometimes within ten or fifteen minutes of giving someone a You Matter bag, I will feel a tap on my shoulder. I turn to see a person in tears asking if they can hug me. Their next question is always, "How did you know?"

How *did* I know they so desperately needed this at a critical moment in their life?

I recently ran into a woman I had once given a You Matter bag to. I never expected to see her again. It was a wonderful surprise, and my heart burst with joy as she shared with me how giving her a You Matter bag impacted her.

Here is what she said in her own words.

Let me start off with saying this happened when I was in Anaheim, California in 2018. At one of my weakest moments of my entire trip, I had just wrapped up a tear fest and was trying my best to dry it up and gather myself together when this woman approached me.

She said, 'Something has pulled me towards you. And someone is telling me you need to know that YOU MATTER.'

She then handed me a lip balm that said YOU MATTER in big black letters and a note card that said the same. On the backside of this card there was a special note that has held massive power not only on that day but in all the days to come.

It read, 'Believe in you and what you can do! Trust in yourself. You are amazing. You are here for a reason. The world needs your light, so shine!'

I quickly canceled my flight that I had just booked to leave this business trip early because I was feeling so low and hopeless, all because of this simple gesture. Because of this random act of kindness, I didn't give up. I didn't let fear consume me. Instead I let it be the power within myself to keep pushing forward.

When I have days of doubt, which let's be real, can be many times in one day or never for an entire week. I would turn to this card. I have it on my fridge still with the lip balm right next to it! I read it more than once a day and it has lifted my spirits many times.

"YOU DO MATTER. Your story does matter," she said. "Who you are today does matter! What you are feeling and going through will become your story. And that my friends will make YOU, you!"

Becca changed my story for me by one simple gesture. She made me rethink my story and helped me realize I can rewrite it at any time. I can become the woman I always wanted to be. Today I can say proudly - I do matter.

It is countless reactions like this one that encourage me to keep stepping out of my comfort zone and keep approaching strangers of all ages and genders. People need to know that others see them and that their presence on this planet matters. When we let others know how much they matter we truly discover how much we matter.

I encourage you to push past any doubts, never second guess or suppress a kind thought.

If you think it or feel it *do it*. Allow yourself the joy and transformation that comes from being a kindness crusader and your life will never be the same again.

BECCA LEVIE is a suicide attempt survivor, storyteller, and is the founder of The LipNotes Foundation and The Yes You Matter movement.

She is CEO of BKNN and a top leader in a direct-sales company where she mentors and motivates a large organization, which sells over 30 million dollars a year in home fragrances. She is the author of *Remember Who You are - Born for Greatness*. Along with being a wife and mother, her passion is awakening audiences to the power of hope and purpose through sharing her own story of trauma turned triumph through what she calls Crap Alchemy.

Connect with Becca
Website: LipNotesFoundation.ORG
Email: Becca@yesyoumatter.org

Week 28

Beginning today, treat everyone you meet as if they were going to be dead by midnight. Extend to them all the care, kindness and understanding you can muster, and do it with no thought of any reward. Your life will never be the same again.

~ Og Mandino

LISTENING WITHOUT JUDGEMENT

There are so many ways for an unplanned act of kindness to manifest. You might take a few extra moments to hold a door open for a stranger at restaurant, or you might simply make eye contact and smile at everyone you walk by, or you might help someone that is struggling get their groceries into their car.

These small acts of kindness can have a much bigger impact than we realize. The personal impact on each of us varies depending on how we receive each experience of kindness. It is not for our own personal accolades or personal gain as the giver. The idea behind a random act of kindness is that it's the unattached intention behind the act of kindness that matters most.

One of the greatest acts of intention-based kindness, however, is to take the time to listen to someone without judgement. This form of kindness is more conscious, has a deeply profound impact, and requires a more concerted focus and sustained effort. It is about holding space for someone else to be who they are.

I hold this act of kindness so sacred because a caring mentor took the time to truly hear and understand me. It was absolutely life changing.

I spent most of my life feeling unheard, unworthy, and I had a low self-esteem, until this amazing woman bestowed upon me her gracious act of kindness. I am so incredibly grateful that this compassionate mentor took the time to listen to me without judgement. This act of kindness is what allowed me to begin to heal and to see value in myself. It completely turned my life around. I now have a confidence that I did not have before. I can share my thoughts with others and not feel at the core level like I have to hide or let the judgement of others stifle me or belittle me. I am able to stand in my own power.

I am always grateful when I have been given the opportunity to listen to someone else without judgement. It is always an opportunity for me to learn and grow as well as to hold a safe space for others to share what is on their minds or question where they are or what paths they are on. The day-to-day life grind and conditioning that we are typically raised with makes it so easy to get in a rut or in a habit of self-imposed limitations that may not serve our highest good.

When we facilitate someone's exploration of paths towards what's possible or into parts of themselves and enable that person to do so without fear of rejection or judgement, it can be a tremendous gift. Just being able to verbalize what is on his or her mind is many times the catalyst of change for that person. So often, it is a change someone wanted to make for a long time but were afraid of what others might think. Instead, she or he would stay stuck. Taking the time to listen and holding space for another person allows that person to start to change how she views herself and different situations. You are letting the person know he is important, she does matter, and he or she is here to share their gifts with others. The world and everyone can benefit from more random and conscious acts of kindness. Share the gift!

DENISE OXLEY uses her creative abilities to invent products for her company. She also does remote healing and clearings on people, pets, properties and businesses. Her goal is to bring healing to millions of people and animals worldwide. She lives in Georgia with her family.

Connect with Denise
Website: deniseoxley.com
Email: denise@deniseoxley.com

Week 29

It's also selfish because it makes you feel good when you help others. I've been helped by acts of kindness from strangers. That's why we're here, after all, to help others.

~ Carol Burnett

MAYBE

I was pregnant with my second daughter when my life turned upside down. I had been experiencing pain, which at times was pretty intense. My obstetrician brushed it off telling me that pain was normal during pregnancy, so I tried to live with it as unbearable as it could be at almost twenty-two weeks of pregnancy. At work one day, I received a panicked call from my perinatologist. I had been required to see her one time because I was considered to be an advanced maternal age. We lived in a small town and her practice was a two-hour drive away. She asked me how I was feeling, and I told her about the pain. Her panic only increased.

She explained that she received a copy of my bloodwork and it was not good. She told me to go to the nearest emergency room and she would send a helicopter for me. My husband drove me to the hospital and from there I was airlifted. When you are airlifted, there is not room for a loved one to ride with you. Even though I arrived at the state-of-the-art children's hospital in thirty minutes, my husband had to drive over two hours to reach me.

True to her word, my doctor was waiting for me when I arrived. They did more testing and my condition rapidly deteriorated. She kept asking when my husband would get there. I envisioned him speeding the windy, unkempt, rural roads and hoped he would make it safely, which he did in half the time it normally would've taken. Once he arrived, the doctor explained I had HELLP Syndrome, a very rare pregnancy complication that can be fatal for mothers. The only way to treat it is to deliver the baby immediately. She estimated that if I didn't deliver then, I would have roughly twenty-four hours to live. Even though we pleaded and prayed, at less than one pound, our baby did not survive.

In the aftermath of the trauma and loss, which is a whole story in itself, we tried to make sense of it all. Now, I am not saying that everything happens for a reason, and that's because I have experienced a tremendous loss that there is no excusable reason for. But there are lessons to be learned in loss. Awhile after our daughter's death, I commented to my husband on how quickly he got to the hospital. He admitted he was driving like a "real a**hole." He said he drove 100 mph, cut people off, and passed when he shouldn't have. We laughed about what the other drivers must have thought of him.

Shortly after this conversation, it clicked. We were driving together in traffic. My husband was driving, and someone cut him off. My husband got angry and was cursing.

I looked at him calmly and intently and said, "Maybe he's on his way to the hospital."

My husband looked back at me and instantly calmed down and chuckled.

"Yeah, maybe," he said.

Driving is a good example because everyone expects all other drivers to be perfect and never make mistakes. Recently, in a span of one week, I was flipped off three times while driving. Two of the times I did absolutely nothing wrong; the other drivers didn't understand the concept of yielding (but, hey maybe their driving instructor skipped that lesson), and the third I was unsure of where to turn and I was driving slowly. Yes, I made a mistake and the driver drove past, flipping me off. What is the point of doing this to people that clearly are already having a difficult time?

My husband and I started to use that phrase a lot and it has worked wonders. Years later we lost a close friendship over a financial issue and I was quite upset.

My husband looked at me and said, "Maybe they are on their way to the hospital."

He was so right. I had no idea what they were going through. Our experience with my pregnancy had shaped us to try and come up with one possible reason why someone would do something and if we could, then we would try our best not to be angry, and instead try to show understanding and kindness. For some reason, our society always looks for people's flaws and mistakes and assumes the worst in everyone. After my experiences, I choose to look for the good and assume the best in others.

Probably much too soon after my loss, I had to go through the painstaking efforts of returning things that I didn't need for my baby. I was in line at department store returning some maternity clothes. I saw a woman who was very pregnant, and she had a little girl. She was looking at a onesie that read,

Little Sister. Telling my daughter that her baby sister had died and dealing with her grief was almost worse than my own, and this onesie really triggered me. I lost it and started crying. Everyone was looking at me, I'm sure wondering, "What the heck is wrong with her?"

Kindness is both an opportunity and a choice. In challenging situations, kindness is not the easy choice to make. Looking back, I can see how incredibly uncomfortable and difficult it must have been for people to choose to be kind to me during my time of tragedy. To the people who dropped off freezer meals, set up a meal train or called me – thank you. To the others who sat with me while I cried or showed up to the hospital and held my baby – thank you. Despite the painful circumstances, you put your feelings aside to reach out to me in my time of sorrow. In my intense grief, these acts of kindness were my solace. During a time when my world was spinning out of control, you were my balance.

Even though it must've been incredibly uncomfortable, these people chose kindness. Acts of kindness, both big and small, were my lifeline.

This kindness that was shown to me, I choose to pay it forward. Please don't think that I am always amazing and kind. I am human. I make mistakes. Big ones sometimes. Everyone you encounter has battles that you know nothing about. Someone didn't smile back at you? Maybe they can't see. Maybe they just found out some horrible news. Maybe her or his heart is broken. If you can come up with one plausible maybe, then choose kindness not judgment. Because maybe your choice of kindness, no matter how small, might mean the world to someone.

TAMARA WEAVER is a licensed clinical social worker and started a non-profit in memory of her daughter Raelyn, Rae of Hope, Inc., which raises funds to assist families with memorial expenses and resources that have suffered from pregnancy infant loss. She lives in California with her husband and three living children who are seven, four, and two.

Connect with Tamara
Website: raeofhopeinc.com
Facebook: raeofhopeincorporated

Week 30

If we're destroying our trees and destroying our environment and hurting animals and hurting one another and all that stuff, there's got to be a very powerful energy to fight that. I think we need more love in the world. We need more kindness, more compassion, more joy, more laughter.

~ Ellen DeGeneres

SPREADING KINDNESS IS AN INSIDE JOB

The greatest act of kindness is the one we provide to ourselves. A simple act of showing compassion and nonjudgment to ourselves is basically spreading kindness in the world by going inward. When we offer kindness in our inner world and find peace internally, we can then bring that peaceful energy to our outer world and contribute to the collective consciousness.

How we feel about ourselves sends out a vibration to the world. The energy can be felt by others. Like some disabilities that cannot be seen by the human eye, some acts of kindness are unseen, but they are felt by those around us. In order to achieve inner peace, we must drop any self-judgement since our thoughts typically cause unnecessary suffering. Many of us think it is selfish to think only about ourselves while easily providing acts of kindness to others. This thought is an example itself of judging our self as wrong and undeserving. The simple act of dropping all self-judgement is the best way to practice self-love therefore, spreading more love into the world.

One of my favorite quotes by Rumi is "Why do you stay in prison when the door is so wide open?"

We could easily ask, "Why do we continue our suffering when we could stop anytime?"

I sometimes say that the root of all suffering in the world is judgement; judgement that my skin color is better than yours; my religion is better than yours; my gender is better than yours, or my country is better than yours. The worst kind of judgment is self-judgement that keeps us locked into the cycle of suffering and beating ourselves up. I also believe that the judgement we put out into the world reflects the self-judgement we are experiencing in our inner world. The judgement that we extend to individuals in our own lives is an extension to the internal suffering that we are choosing to allow in our inner world. Emotional suffering is optional in life and I have been looking at ways I can let myself off the hook, so I can move internally closer to peace.

I'm pretty good about not judging actions of what people do in their lives, since I can see the highest good that is happening even in the perceived bad events in life. I know and trust that everything is working *for* us and not *to* us. All our experiences are helping the expansion of our souls and pushing us closer to something that is yet to be known but will bring us more joy. Holding space for others means having the ability to see the higher vision of who they are – their truth. For me this means not judging a friend and the life experiences they are choosing since it is the perfect journey for their soul.

Although we may use different names for it, I believe that everyone is on a spiritual path. The universe is supporting each of us as we have our unique experiences. We all hike the same trail differently. I might stop at each bolder to sit. A friend might go the whole distance without stopping. We all eventually end up at the same place.

I had an awakening in my late forties when I started to go spiritual events and attend trainings. All my friends were very surprised since all my beliefs shifted. Some friends also feared that I might move on from our friendships because of all the changes happening in my life. I was afraid that people I loved might go out of my life. My self-judgements were causing me a lot of suffering.

Recently the universe gave me an opportunity to practice sharing loving self-kindness and choosing to stop the suffering when I was stuck in a cycle of life was happening to me. I have a dear friend that I love very much, and I was finding it hard to hold space and allow her to have her life experience. Although she was unaware, I attached my wellbeing to her actions and caused myself emotional suffering losing my inner peace. With this one friend, I could not just let her hike the trail her way, and I kept trying to have her take my exact spiritual path. I would also take time to reflect on the mirror she shined into my life. Yet I spent so much time trying to help her walk beside me on the trail that I took it personally when she made other choices. This added more suffering into my well-being. I couldn't understand why I was doing this since I really accept everyone's life choices. I was trying to figure out why I took so much responsibility for her journey. One reason was the fear of someone going out of my life. However, the choices she made were perfect for her and she was happy. I was actually causing myself suffering by "judging" my judgement of her path, which would eventually turn into resentment.

While in Hawaii attending a healing event with Michael Tamura, I was able to focus on releasing the energy of responsibility for others that holds me back from living fully in my power. After doing that work and forgiving myself of all the judgement, especially the self-judgements, I was able to shift my energy with this friend. Please note that I did not say *she* had to change or do something to shift the energy, but that *I* took responsibility for my suffering. We get to choose how we feel. We create the energy that moves us through our life. So, if you're experiencing suffering in your life, then look at your energy around the situation. Best thing to do is to drop the self-judgement and practice self-love and self-kindness. The peace we create internally by being gentler on ourselves is the best way to spread kindness in the world.

How we feel inside is felt by those around us. This is especially true for empaths who will feel it quite deeply. The kindest thing we can do for the world is to be happy and have internal peace.

Sometimes it is hard for us to see all the specific causes for our suffering, but typically it stems from fear. The closer we move towards our truth, which is love, then the energy will shift. All I know for sure is that I am not going to judge anything about others, and especially not judge myself. Spreading kindness is an inside job.

PAULA OBEID shares love with the world as a master hypnotherapist and NATH transpersonal hypnotherapy trainer, Reiki Master, bestselling author, and intuitive life and business coach. She motivates and facilitates individuals that are ready to create change in their lives.

Utilizing proven effective strategies and modalities, Paula aids people in achieving their business and personal goals. Her successful, compassionate approach utilizes intuition, reflective listening skills, training on various modalities, and knowledge gained from her life experiences. Paula's passions are reflected in her heart-centered endeavors that provide services, education, and products that allow individuals to lovingly move through life with joy and ease.

Connect with Paula
Website: blissalways.com
Website: pureathome.com

Week 31

Constant kindness can accomplish much. As the sun makes ice melt, kindness causes misunderstanding, mistrust, and hostility to evaporate.

~ Albert Schweitzer

DREAMS COME TRUE WHEN SUPPORTED BY KINDNESS

I've always had a passion for creating things. Ever since we were younger, my sister Sophia and I have always loved to film movies and funny videos. Back in January, our parents finally let us start our own YouTube channel. We've been posting comedy videos every week since then and have gained over eight-hundred subscribers already. Making videos has taught us to be ourselves and not care what anyone else thinks of us. YouTube has given us the outlet to express our weird personalities and make other people laugh. Most parents think YouTube is stupid and they don't get it, but our parents have been very supportive of our channel, and I'm really grateful that they go out of their way to help with our videos.

Since our channel is soon to hit 1,000 subscribers, Sophia and I decided to film a movie to release to our channel. The main message of the movie was going to be about embracing your inner-weirdness and not caring about other people's opinions of you. This was going to be our best video yet, and my main summer project. I worked on the script for about a month, and we worked so hard to gather a cast for the movie. I even had to meet with the principal to discuss the project and reserve the school to film some scenes. The day before filming, I was super stressed out. I had over fifteen people coming to be in the movie, and I didn't know how I could possibly manage everyone. Thankfully, the day went pretty smoothly, and we got the first couple of scenes done in two hours. I was so relieved it was over, and I couldn't wait to get home and edit the footage I had.

A week later, we had a couple of people over to film one of our weekly videos. When I opened the video camera to start filming, a message appeared on the screen. It said I had inserted the memory card the wrong way. I didn't think much of it and I flipped the card around and put it in the other way. The message showed up again. I tried to reinsert the card every possible way I could, and the message didn't go away.

It was then I realized something was seriously wrong with the card.

I went to plug it into my computer where I do my editing, and my computer didn't even recognize it. I went into full-panic mode because I had hours of footage from the movie on that card. Then the worst-case scenario came through my mind. If I couldn't get that footage back, I would have to cancel the movie. We had only filmed the first few scenes of the movie, but there was no way I could get all of those people together to film at the school again. It was stressful enough the first time.

I searched online for every possible thing that could be wrong with the card and nothing worked. I ended up calling my dad and he told me to leave it alone until he got home from work. I left it alone, but I couldn't relax knowing that everything I had ever filmed on that camera was completely gone.

When my dad got home, after hours at work, he tried to see what was wrong with it. After about half an hour, it was no use. He explained to me how I had corrupted the card by just pulling it out of my computer instead of properly ejecting it through settings. That's when it all made sense. So that's what that "Be Careful" alert meant on my computer whenever I took out the card. It was warning me about corrupting my data.

He couldn't find any way to retrieve the data on the memory card. I was about to lose all hope and make the final decision to cancel the movie when he finally came up with a solution. He found a way to transfer all the files I needed to his flash-drive from work. Even though I had all the footage I needed, my memory card still wouldn't work with the video camera. My dad went out of the way to buy me a brand new memory card, which is not cheap.

Because of his act of kindness, I have everything back on track for the movie, and I hope to finish it soon. I am very grateful for my dad and all that he has done for me. If it wasn't for him, I would have had to cancel the whole movie. Even after a long day at work, he came home and fixed my memory card that I had broken. I am also thankful for the support my family has given for my YouTube channel and for my passion for filmmaking. Countless amounts of times, my mom has taken me out of her way to places like the mall and the school to film. She has also agreed to be in a lot of my weird videos knowing that hundreds of people would see it. Without the support and kindness of my family, I wouldn't be where I am today: making videos, doing what I love.

VALERIE LARSON is a high school student from Michigan. She is an artist, illustrator, author, and YouTuber. She has been drawing since she was five years old and still loves it. She enjoys making short films and comedy videos on her YouTube channel, Nosral Studios, with her sister, Sophia. Valerie hopes to find a career in film someday.

Connect with Valerie
YouTube: Nosral Studios
Instagram: Nosral Studios
Facebook: Nosral Studios

Week 32

The best portion of a good man's life is his little, nameless, unremembered acts of kindness and of love.

~ William Wordsworth

KINDNESS MY STRENGTH

I remember the feeling of the cold coffee can on my bum as I squatted to poo in the dark of the night. I pulled up my tattered, little-girl panties and quietly crawled back into the van, I could feel the floor beneath me, and bits of dirt stuck to my skin. I brushed them off and curled into a ball. The darkness was like a blanket around me. I tried to breathe as quietly as possible so as not to wake my father. I felt that if I could be still enough, then I could disappear.

Images from my nightmares flooded my mind. The fear built within me to the point where I just cried. I could rush into the arms of my daddy and feel safe, but I knew that immediate relief from this night terror would come with a price, hugs and cuddles always did, especially in the darkness of the night.

As a child, there was rarely a true escape from nightmares. I don't know what was worse: the monsters in my dreams or the monsters in my life. Genuine kindness was not something that I often experienced growing up. Still, I felt as though I would search the ends of the earth to find it, I could feel it inside me: a deep care for living things. I'd gather the bugs I called roly-polies that were curled into balls under the stones outside and then bring them water and grass. I would lose myself in their world. How lucky they were. They were never alone, and any time that they didn't want to be touched, they could lock themselves up in a ball that even the most prying hands couldn't open. When children cried and animals whimpered, I could feel it in my heart. No matter how absent kindness seemed to be in my world, I knew it must exist because I could feel it within me.

"Certainly, I mustn't be the only one. Surely, there are others out there like me," I thought.

Heart wide-open, I searched for kindness in the eyes of strangers, hoping for a glimmer of light. With one simple smile, I found encouragement, warmth, and even hope.

I could see the shining lights of homes and porchlights as my father drove in the night, the van was our moving home but I so longed to know what it was like to live in a *real* home. I watched the grandmas and the grandpas sit on the porch. If I got lucky, then I would catch a glimpse of a mom setting the table or a dad watering the grass while kids and or animals happily played by their side. In these moments, I found a place to belong. Each glimpse suspended in my mind like sunshine at the end of a dark tunnel. It was a distant hope to one day to know the kindness I saw in the world.

I'd watch all the people in their cars, I was fascinated by other lifestyles and incredibly curious. I was also incredibly desperate to make a connection outside the confines of what felt like a very tragic reality. Eager to make eye contact, I was thrilled when we hit traffic. As the drivers busied themselves with the stress of making it to the next destination, I reveled in the chance to make a connection with kids in the backseats. I'd see an older teen girl or a kid my age and hope for eye contact. I was always ready to give my best smile and send as much love as a kind look could give. Occasionally, I would get a smile back. It would light up my whole day! I was always searching for any remnant of kindness and any gesture gave me hope – no matter how big or small.

I came to a crossroad, after years of childhood trauma, schoolyard bullying, and sexual assault, I began to question the value of kindness. I began to wonder if my kindness was my weakness. There seemed to be an air of strength carried by the hard hearted. I thought of all that I'd lost through the years, the things personally lost or taken by those less sensitive, less kind, and seemingly empowered by a lack of caring. I began to list the lost things: my mom, my dad, my clothes, my teddy bear, and memorabilia. Then I listed all the things that have been stolen from me: money, a pet bird, clothes, and even underwear! The list went on: my virginity, my childhood.

I couldn't bear to think of one more thing. Tears began to roll down my face. In that moment of despair, I suddenly had a thought that would change my life forever, "Of all the things that could be lost, there is was one thing that no one could ever take from me. My heart."

My thoughts shifted to those people who were kind to me, the housemother in the girls' shelter who believed in me, the friend who searched me out as I bounced through foster homes, and the school counselor who inspired me to finish high school. Simple kindness of the few fueled my heart with hope that lit my way in the darkest moments of my life. I wiped my tears and took a deep breath. As my lungs filled with life giving air, I felt my heart open and release. It was in that moment that I decided to carry the torch. Committed to keep my heart soft, it was then that kindness became forever my strength.

MELANIE MORRISON of Sacred Shifts LLC is a Let Your Yoga Dance teacher, professional angel card reader, public speaker, and humanitarian. She is passionate about helping people shift their energies and mindsets by connecting to the rhythm of nature's cycles through music and movement.

Using cards, she guides clients through the deepest waters of the heart and helps them clear blocks to reach their highest potentials! Her Sacred Shifts circles and classes empower everyone to connect to their inner guidance leading them to lives full of freedom, purpose and joy!

To book for public speaking or reading text or call the number below.

Connect with Melanie
Website: sacredshifts.org
Facebook: SacredShifts1
Instagram: sacredshifts
Phone: 808-397-6941

Week 33

Kindness is a passport that opens doors and fashions friends. It softens hearts and molds relationships that can last lifetimes.

~ Joseph B. Wirthlin

KINDNESS LAID THE FOUNDATION FOR MY EXISTENCE

Writing a piece in this book is a great adventure for me. When I set out on a new adventure, I start with the basics. If I'm going to write about kindness, then I need to know its official definition. The Merriam-Webster definition of kind is "having or showing a friendly, generous, and considerate nature." The definition makes me think of my parents. Two major instances of kindness have transformed my life and they are both related to my family. The first act of kindness was shown by a woman I've never met – my biological mother.

I don't know the circumstances of my conception. I don't know whether the sexual intimacy between my biological parents included love, lust, adventure, joy, or anything even remotely positive. The details of my birth parents are a mystery that I have chosen to respect. What I do know is that my birth mother faced a decision regarding her pregnancy and ultimately chose to carry and care for me for nine months before placing me for adoption with a reputable agency.

I am forever grateful to my birth mother for the act of kindness that gave me life. I cannot fathom the challenges she faced when confronted with a decision to give birth and then place me up for adoption. I don't know the kind of resistance she managed along with the internal changes in her body. I empathize with the many women facing the same decision. Because of the statistics of abortions in the United States, I realize that my situation could have easily been different.

The second act of kindness that transformed my life was when I was adopted. Three months after I was born, an American couple said yes to adopting me despite not matching my ethnic heritage. I am Mexican-American and was born with thick black hair that stood up in the back due to a cowlick. My mother is German-American and Hungarian-American and my father is Italian-American and they loved me as their own. They annoy people with their endless praise of my activities, which they are always quick to relay to strangers.

I felt so loved and cherished that it never occurred to me that I was adopted even though they told me daily. They were advised to make it common knowledge that I was adopted to prevent my adoption from being a family secret. In elementary school, I failed a vision test. The evaluator asked me whether either of my parents wore glasses. Without hesitation, I affirmed that my mother wore glasses.

When I recounted the story, at the dinner table, my mom started to cry. She was touched by the realization that I did not see a separation of what biological or DNA gave me to what she had given me. Their love for me could not be more intense or comprehensive if my mother had carried me in her body. They've given of themselves throughout my childhood and well into my adulthood. My father spent time with me through participation in father-and-daughter organizations and events. My mom taught me to cook, clean, decorate for the seasons, and entertain. She had a well-chosen group of friends who have been the bedrock of my upbringing. One of her friends became my cherished godmother and another unfailingly celebrates my birthday and wedding anniversary. She would spend hours helping me find clothing that fit my body and would put all discarded outfits back on hangars.

Throughout my entire life, their actions consistently reflect their love for me and still do. We love spending time together. As I aged, they morphed from parents into best friends and they've lovingly embraced my husband in the same fashion that they adopted me. They are our favorite double-date partners. They provided a home, love, and blessed life to me, a child that had been given up for adoption. Their legacy of kindness has transformed my life.

TONI BRUCATO-KOBET loves breaking the stereotype of a yoga teacher. Those who think they are too old, too inflexible, or too out of shape to practice yoga will see that if Toni can do it then so can they. Toni has always considered herself to be a healer and gives people permission to rest and practice self-care.

The quieter your mind becomes, the more profoundly your life energy is restored. She is certified with Yoga Alliance, certified to facilitate Yoga Nidra through the Amrit Institute, and loves leading vision-board workshops.

Connect with Toni B
Website: Tonibyoga.com
Email: toni@tonibyoga.com
Instagram: drtbk
Instagram: Tonibdiscover
Facebook: Toni B Yoga
LinkedIn: Toni B Yoga
Twitter: Toni B Yoga1
Pinterest: Toni B Yoga
Phone: 480-330-4018

Week 34

You don't teach morals and ethics and empathy and kindness in the schools. You teach that at home, and children learn by example.

~ Judy Sheindlin

THE KINDNESS OF A STRANGER

We never know when we will become dependent on a stranger until all our trust is placed in one.

Most of my life I have been an independent woman and single mother to two children and our lives were spent on the go. I worked full- time as a registered dental assistant in pediatrics while attending night school to become an emergency medical technician, both children played multiple sports and I was given full physical custody when the children's father moved out of state, which happened when they were two and four years old. It was never an option for me to get sick, injured or to not be 100 percent available physically or emotionally. Thankfully, God gave me the strength to keep getting up when life would knock me down.

On the days leading up to depending on the kindness of a stranger, I often walked my children to their classrooms on beautifully crisp December mornings. Mornings in northern California are clear and can be icy but it was not the ice that challenged me. During those mornings the sun was piercing bright as it came over the rooftops of the school buildings. Many times I had to close one eye to see where I was going.

When we were walking to my daughter's classroom that Friday there was a straight shot to the classroom door. The sun glared into my eyes while my daughter held my hand. The next Monday I took my son to his class first, and my daughter and I repeated the same route to her classroom but this time something was in the way!

Squinting into the sun I saw the rooftops and said to myself "Just keep walking straight and you will find the door." Next thing I know I was airborne and my daughter was screaming "Mommy!, Mommy!" I landed flat on my back. I just laid there stunned asking myself what just happened?

My daughter was upset and I told her "I'm fine and Mommy needs to rest after going boom."

I was dazed, couldn't breathe. There was pain in the back of my head and neck. The piercing sun was still beating into my eyes. I lay motionless and calm because during my emergency medical training I had been learning to never move someone who had fallen especially someone with possible neck and back injuries. While still lying on the cold December pavement, I convinced my daughter she could walk to her classroom by herself which she did obediently.

As the wind returned to my lungs and I began to access what happened I noticed none of the other parents were stopping to help me.

No one asked me "Why are you laying on the ground?"

Parents and children continued to walk around me, saying nothing, which made me feel invisible.

I was on the ground for at least ten minutes when a man offered to help me. I couldn't see him because he was behind me but his voice was calm and kind. He asked if I needed an ambulance. I wasn't sure. We spoke for several more minutes and I decided calling an ambulance to the school was too much drama; it would upset the children who might watch from the classroom windows.

I switched into thinking about what the emergency medical technicians would do for me if called out. I used my trauma skill training on myself! I knew what the day and date was, my name and where I was. I was breathing so I had a working airway. The pain in the back of my head was lessening, but my neck was still sore. I could feel no broken or protruding bones. Nothing felt wet and warm so no bleeding. I could feel and move all my fingers and toes without numbness. I decided it was okay to move *slowly*.

Rolling onto my side, I kept my neck straight until I came up onto my knees. Upright and kneeling, I couldn't believe my eyes; the calm and kind man that stayed with me and talking to me was in a wheelchair!

I started crying.

I knew why he was the one helping me. I bet that he knew what it was like to be scared; he knew what it was like to feel invisible; he knew what it was like to feel helpless. I bet that he knew what it was like to feel dependent on someone else for comfort. He also likely knew what it was like to have a sudden and unavoidable accident!

He was familiar to me as a parent but I didn't know which children were his or how he came to be in a wheelchair. He seemed genuinely at peace and accepting his situation and that helped me in mine.

Through my tears, I repeatedly said "Thank you."

He encouraged me to get checked out medically. I asked him if he saw what had happened because I still couldn't make sense of how I ended up in the air and landed flat on my back! He said that over the previous weekend parents had volunteered for the school clean-up day and some benches were donated. It was a new bench that I went up and over. I looked to his right and sure enough, a brand-new shiny enamel green-painted bench was right in the path of where I had just walked! I wondered how I could have missed that, but I'd been looking straight ahead into the bright sun and not downward.

On that crisp day in December 2003 the kindness of a stranger taught me compassion, patience, empathy, listening and to let someone decide for themselves what they need in a time of crisis. He allowed me stay in control when I felt scared and out of control. He let me figure out what I needed and in that moment? I needed to not feel alone.

When I worked with my patients and clients, I emulated the gifts he gave to me whether I was on duty as a Sonoma County EMT for eleven years and when I was a registered dental assistant for thirty years. I still do it now as a certified energy medicine practitioner since 2013.

For me, the acts of listening and finding a balance where someone feels both safe and heard in a time of crisis is kindness. Opening our hearts and stepping into the other person's shoes for that brief period of time is invaluable because their current reality is anything but kind. We can be unkind to our bodies physically; we can be unkind to ourselves with our words and emotions and we can be unkind spiritually when we starve ourselves of love. When we are kind to ourselves, we come from a place of love that spills over to others. The kindness of a stranger taught me to be kind to myself so I am now ready and able to serve others through my kindness just as he did for me.

ANNEMARIE LAFFERTY, CECP, RDA and retired emergency medical technician, intuitively guides clients to achieve inner peace while quieting the mind and body since 2013. Annemarie's clinical experience includes twenty-five years as registered dental assistant in pediatrics, eighteen years as a non-RN operating room scrub nurse and eleven years as a Sonoma Co. emergency medical technician.

Ms. Lafferty owns Greater Awareness Energy Medicine and Healing Within Wellness Sprays in Petaluma, California. She is a programmer for KPCA 103.3FM weekly radio talk-show "Healing Within" and the producer and director of "Healing Within" television shows.

Connect with Annemarie
Website: healingwithin.us
Email: healingwithin11@gmail.com
Facebook: Annemarielafferty
Instagram: greater_awareness_energy

Week 35

Guard well within yourself that treasure, kindness. Know how to give without hesitation, how to lose without regret, how to acquire without meanness.

~ George Sand

KINDNESS AND THE POWER OF LOVING INTENTION

Do you have a strong desire to do good, but you get overwhelmed because the need is so great? Do you get discouraged because you feel you don't have the time, money, and resources needed to make an impact? Sometimes we may feel insignificant. We feel that what we have to offer isn't enough to really make a difference, but that couldn't be further from the truth. Every action, every thought, and every intention you initiate affects the whole of humanity and the expansion of the universe. Make no mistake, Kindness Crusader, you are more powerful than you know, and you possess everything you will ever need to impact all of humanity in a great way.

The True Nature of Kindness

Once you understand the true nature of kindness, there is no limit to the good you can do. Kindness is generally defined as the demonstration of the qualities of being friendly, generous, and considerate through words or actions. Many would agree that this is an acceptable and logical definition of kindness, but if we delve deeper, we find there is more to it than meets the eye.

Are you familiar with the esoteric wisdom of "as above, so below?" If you are like me, you know that there is more to life than what we physically experience in our everyday. This is just one reality. Besides our physical plane, we are also connected to the spiritual plane. Both planes mirror each other but operate differently. Instead of the tangible objects we experience in this physical plane, the spiritual plane consists of the energetic, vibrational component to our earthly experiences.

Whew! That can be a lot if you are new to these concepts but think about it in this way. Whatever you do on earth takes place energetically on the spiritual plane, and the vibration of whatever transpires on the spiritual plane affects you here on earth.

So, what does this have to do with kindness? Think of kindness as a coin with two sides. The earthly side and the spiritual side. An earthly act of kindness may be experienced as a smile, a helping hand, kind word, touch, or any observable act of love. Every earthly act of kindness has a mirroring vibrational spiritual component. An earthly act of kindness is powerful, but the corresponding spiritual vibration of that earthly act is where the true impact of kindness is felt. The loving thoughts, intentions, and positive emotion behind the observable act have more of an impact than the act itself.

The Big Picture

As a Kindness Crusader, it is crucial that you understand the implications of the vibrational nature of kindness. When you realize that you can perform acts of kindness with your thoughts and pure positive intention with or without tangible action, you understand that you can help anyone at any time and change any circumstance for the better. It's not the money you give or the amount of time you spend. It's not your ability to say all the right words or the helping hand you are able to lend. If you have these things to give? That's wonderful! They are kind and loving gestures, but they are not where the true power of kindness lies. If you have none of these things to offer, do not be discouraged because the true power of kindness lies in your loving thoughts and the focused, positive attention you send out into the world.

Take the time today to sit and think about the things you would like to see changed for the better, the people you would like to help, and the wounds within yourself that you are still working to heal. Hold it all in the highest of your intention and send it out lovingly into the Universe. The Universe will back you in a powerful way and expand your kindness to touch the world in ways beyond what you can imagine. Your intentions cause a point of vibration that radiates out into the universe affecting all of existence; facilitating expansion, growth, knowledge, and love as it radiates through the collective consciousness of all of humanity. Ultimately returning to you and manifesting in your physical experience will be the karma of magnified love and good fortune from the most unexpected and delicious places.

Your intentional act of kindness achieved through your loving thoughts raises the vibration of everyone and contributes to making the world a better place.

Kindness Crusader, I thank you for your courage, strength, and kind heart. I extend to you peace, blessings and all my love as you use your power of kindness in all its forms to make the universe a better place.

Namaste.

ERICA PEACE is a natural intuitive who is passionate about helping others prosper, grow, and heal through her multidisciplinary integrative, energy practice. Besides having a degree in interpersonal communication, Erica has certifications in yoga, personal training, nutritional therapy and therapeutic bodywork. In addition, she has been attuned and trained as a master energy healer and elite life coach.

Erica has always been fascinated with quantum theory, spirituality, and all things metaphysical. She loves to share her knowledge of these subjects through writing, speaking, and teaching. When not working, you can find Erica hiking or hanging out with her two amazing sons.

Connect with Erica
Website: Metalifemastery.com
Email: erica@metalifemastery.com

Week 36

For beautiful eyes, look for the good in others; for beautiful lips, speak only words of kindness; and for poise, walk with the knowledge that you are never alone.

~ Audrey Hepburn

WANTED: SMILES & EYEBALLS

Kindness comes in packages of all sizes. It doesn't matter if it's a split-second, smiling greeting, holding the door for someone, paying for a cup of coffee, or organizing a fundraiser; kindness offers an opportunity for both the giver and the receiver to commune with one another. Humans are communal by nature. When we're having an off, bad, or even terrible day because of hurt, anger, frustration, or overwhelming stress, we tend to feel isolated. One single act of kindness helps us feel not so alone.

Often, the worse we feel, the more impact a simple act of kindness will have on us.

Here's a key piece to keep in mind, we don't know what another person is struggling with because it doesn't always reflect in their demeanor or actions. Some people are really good at covering up their pain.

Smiles are a universal language which invoke an echoing gesture in return. As soon as I decided to join this beautiful Kindness Crusader project, an image of an older gentleman passing me by on the street flashed through my mind. His eyes met mine, fingers going to the brim of his hat, he nodded and smiled as he passed me by. You know the feeling. It was that old-movie, wholesome, feel-good feeling. It made me smile in turn, warmed my heart to know that there are good people like that coexisting in the world.

That smile told me, "Hello."

It said, "Good Day."

It meant, "Nice to see you."

It said, "You matter."

Then reality kicked in and it made me sad for the current and upcoming generations. As wonderful as technology is as it allows so many connections, social mannerisms and the art of conversation – both with words and body language – is fading away. The simplest acts of kindness are fading along with it. Don't get me wrong, I use emojis and bitmojis in the technological world. Truth be told, I enjoy them.

They allow for some personality to show through, but nothing, I repeat *nothing*, replaces a friendly, real-life smile!

If you think about it, it isn't even possible to smile at someone without looking at them. Ah, there's another social mannerism fading away. Eye contact. What could offer you a sense of belonging more than eye contact?

It means, "I see you and I acknowledge you."

It means, "You exist. I exist. We exist together."

It means, "You aren't alone."

All these thoughts are mirrored to us when eye contact is coupled with even the slightest of smiles.

When my daughter was first diagnosed with bipolar disorder, she was hospitalized while they worked with medications to bring her balance. She was frightened and felt very alone. One of the things that helped her work through her emotions was writing poetry.

Here is one of her entries:

"Please" by Holly Cockerham
As the days pass by slow
My thoughts start to flow
As anxiety makes them race
My heart can't keep a steady pace
Trying to be calm
I frantically scratch at my palm
I'll never be at peace
If my mind won't ease
So give me a smile
Just one
I'm Begging
Please

It is my personal opinion that this poem speaks volumes about compassion, kindness and the primal need for positive human interaction. We truly will never know the impact a simple act of kindness, such as a smile, can have on others. Even if you are in a position that cares for others as a job or career, I invite you to not allow yourself to be caught up in the to-do's and stress of the position and forget to remember why you chose to be there in the first place – your 'why.'

Compassion comes from your kindness muscle and is so vital to the receiver. A smile costs nothing and requires little effort. The impact of having that eye contact when paying forward a smile is priceless. Again, I refer to the poem above, which I am sure speaks on behalf of all who find themselves struggling. It makes me sad that society doesn't normally lend itself to support or encourage others to reach out and ask for help. I find it uplifting and a step in the right direction that there are crusaders in the world seeking to catalyze change. We don't have to be a British royal to be a Kindness Crusader; we just have to be caring individuals who are willing to pay forward a kindness. Every smile makes a difference. Be that difference!

When you are down, having others send a smile your way makes a difference. When you are having a truly bodacious day, you cannot help but smile. That feeling can be as contagious as a yawn. To add even more positivity to this state of being, you will never know what a positive impact you will have on other people's day as a result of paying forward one simple act of kindness. The next time you are feeling on top of the world, don't feel guilty about it or keep it to yourself, spread that joy!

Kindness leads to compassion, which forges a foundation that communities can be built upon, communities that exist for the betterment and wellbeing of all. I double-dog dare you, dear Kindness Crusader to a challenge. Yep, you guessed it. It's a kindness challenge. Over the next thirty days, make it a priority to don your kindness cape and spread your kindness superpower!

CRYSTAL COCKERHAM is an author, mentor, and feminine wisdom teacher. Crystal works with women to guide them through the spiritual alchemical process of transformation in order to be liberated from the world's perceptions.

Using her own special blend of spiritual midwifery, Crystal guides women through the process of transformation, forging, and solidifying their innate connections to their inner wisdom, allowing them to access their own truth, empowering them to claim their sovereignty and become the women they are truly meant to be so they can live a more connected, joy-filled life. To begin your journey, and find out more, visit her website.

Connect with Crystal
Website: WisdomAwakens.com

Week 37

First and foremost, we need to be the adults we want
our children to be. We should watch our own gossiping
and anger. We should model the kindness we want to see.

~ Brene Brown

THE SEED OF KINDNESS

What kind of world are we leaving our children?

I know that I am not the only parent that worries about our children and the future generations. Every time you turn on the television, you are bombarded with images and stories of loss, murder, theft, war, disease. The list goes on and on. So, what can we do? How do we solidify the possibility of a brighter, kinder future for our children?

My oldest, Nikola, has a heart of gold and I pray he never loses it. A couple of years ago, when he was about three years old, I witnessed a moment that gave me a glimmer of hope for our future generations.

I was in the kitchen throwing dinner in the crockpot while simultaneously playing with Nikola. "Mama, can I have some money?" he asked.

"Why, kiddo?"

"Pretend money, Mama."

I hand him some pretend money. He precedes to toss the pretend money into the air.

"More. Please?" he asked.

I handed him some more money, and he tossed it again. This went on a couple of more times.

I had to ask. "I know this is pretend money, but, dude, why are you tossing it all away?"

"Mama, some peoples might need it more."

"Really?"

"Yes. Not all peoples have money, Mama. We share."

I was fist pumping, raising the roof, patting myself on the back and possibly taking a bow in my kitchen. You see, he had to be getting that from somewhere and don't get me wrong. I'm not trying to toot my own horn because it's not just me.

Recently a neighbor about one street over lost their entire home to a fire. When my husband saw what happened, he stopped by to see if they could use some assistance. Food, water, anything.

"What can we do?" he asked.

Our boys witnessed that. It's so very true when people say that children watch what you do more closely than they listen to what you say.

Not too long ago, Nikola's school had a build-a-bear truck set up at his pre-k. I had given him the money to make a bear that morning. It was about $25-30. When I picked him up that afternoon, I commented on his bear and he was unusually quiet, looking down on the ground.

I asked him what was wrong, and he responded, "Mama, I'm not sure everyone got a bear."

We discussed that a bit and then he got extremely serious.

"Mama, can we go give the school some money for the afternoon class?"

I didn't even hesitate. I turned the truck around, and we walked back into the school. Come to find out, a lot of teachers and a couple of local businesses had donated some money to make sure every child *could* make a bear. Once this was confirmed by his principal, Nikola was content enough to head home.

What can we do to make this world better? It's the little things. The choices we make daily. Do we buy that extra burger and give it to the man on the corner? Do we donate our unused clothes or toys that our kids no longer play with? Do we give to food drives? Do we volunteer our time?

Allow your children to see little rosebuds of kindness in your daily choices.

What can you do for the future of your children? The concept is simple. Start planting seeds of kindness in the hearts of your children. The hope lies within them.

Water the next generation.

Ways to Model Kindness and Get Your Children Involved

♥ Grab a snack that gives back for every sale made.

♥ Hand out granola bars or any type of snack to the homeless.

♥ Buy an extra burger for that guy standing outside of the burger place. Not sure that he would take it from you? Ask an employee at the restaurant to take it out to him.

♥ Buy a family some groceries and leave it on the family's doorstep.

♥ Donate your clothes that you aren't wearing anymore. Donate your kid's toys that they don't play with anymore.

♥ Donate to a food drive.

♥ Volunteer at a soup kitchen.

♥ Hold the door open for a stranger.

♥ Help put the groceries on the conveyor belt for the mommy at the grocery store with her hands full with children. Offer to help unload them for her.

♥ Help an elderly person grab something from a top shelf.

♥ Smile and do it often. A smile has the power to change the world, one person at a time.

♥ Give firm handshakes and powerful hugs. Look people in the eyes. Show respect.

♥ Turn your back on the idea that it's cool to be aloof, detached, or unemotional. Show the world that it is important to be heartfelt and kind.

♥ Sincerely thank the people that assist you in your daily life, no matter how big or small.

♥ Lead by example.

♥ Remain positive. Keep your head up.

♥ Complain less. Praise more.

♥ Apologize when needed and mean it.

♥ Forgive, yourself and others.

♥ Stand up for others.

♥ Remain thankful, even in the dark times.

♥ Never be too busy to help a friend or family member.

♥ Make time for what you love and believe in.

♥ Believe in the goodness of people. Believe that people really can make a difference.

LANA PUMMILL is a wife and mother to two little boys, ages five and three. Her tank is fueled by coffee, hugs, giggles, and lots of wet kisses. Her days are spent dodging Nerf bullets, jumping over little cars, cleaning up spills, wiping runny noses, washing a million loads of laundry a day, and that is only the beginning.

Lana says, "I had forgotten who I was. So to find myself again, I started writing again. I invite you to come along with me. Let's laugh. Let's cry. Let's dream, inspire, and grow together."

Connect with Lana
Website: findinginspirationinthechaos.blog
Facebook: findinginspirationinthechaos
Pinterest: lanapummill
Instagram: lanapummill
Twitter: LanaPummill
Linkedin: lanapummill

Week 38

That best portion of a man's life, his little, nameless,

unremembered acts of kindness and love.

~ William Wordsworth

WWLD … WHAT WOULD LIZZIE DO?
THE KINDNESS OF LIZZIE

My son Ryan has had many trials and tribulations in his thirty-three years. The one thing that Ryan always wanted was to have someone special, to have his own family. Eventually, he met Lizzie.

"Elisabeth with an "s," he told me at the beginning of their relationship.

I was so excited and had a great feeling about Lizzie. We met after a few weeks and they were officially a couple. That's when I knew it was serious. He added her information to his Facebook page … I know … *really* serious. We met her family. It wasn't long before they announced that a baby was on the way.

Both families were excited. This baby would be both of our respective families fourth grandchild. Lizzie's pregnancy went by quickly with only a few bumps in the road. We found out in a reveal party that we would be welcoming a little boy into our families. The baby was due around my birthday in October. On October 19, ten days after my birthday, Lizzie went into labor. I got the phone call from Ryan to get ready to come over; a short time later I received another phone call and was told to come now because there was a problem.

When I arrived at the hospital, Ryan was crying and walking toward me with the doctor. Unfortunately, Lizzie's labor had become complicated and unstable because of a blood-related issue; leukemia. She was being transfused, and things were not looking good. When I went in to see her, she introduced me as her mother-in-law just to make me feel better and establish our relationship. It was so kind. They eventually stabilized her, and my healthy grandson Nathan was delivered by Caesarean Section. Lizzie was unable to hold her son until two days later due to transfusions and complications. I never heard her complain. The hospital allowed Nathan and Ryan to stay in her room for the first five or six days while the doctors were waiting for Lizzie to recover and before beginning her first round of chemo. Lizzie's mom took Nathan home to care for him and was helped by some of Lizzie's siblings.

The rest of us either rotated to visit Lizzie or the baby. Everyone pooled their money and time to make sure that all areas of their lives were looked after.

During the first round of chemo, Lizzie spent over thirty days in the hospital. She was allowed to go home and spend time with her family for about seven days. She'd return to the hospital for inpatient chemo and monitoring for five more rounds of chemo. The plan was for her to be completely cancer free and find a 100 percent match for a bone marrow transplant to have her best chance of survival. Her siblings went for testing, and we anxiously awaited the results. One of her siblings was a perfect match!

About the time that she was to go for the bone marrow transplant, she became ill and had to wait. Then, she had to go through another round of chemo. Shortly after that, she awoke to find a bump on her forehead that turned out to be cancer. It was found in different spots in her body. Unfortunately, Lizzie carried the Philadelphia chromosome, which keeps the cancer cells for leukemia activated. She had been on medication that was supposed to turn the cells off, but it wasn't working for her the way it did for most people.

The doctors decided to send her to Houston to a famous cancer center so she could be considered for a clinical trial that included a different drug to try to manage the chromosome. Lizzie and Ryan went; she had all of the tests, but ultimately decided to have the drug administered from here in Phoenix where they lived. Her family and support system and her new baby were all in Phoenix.

A new plan was made. She would receive chemo at home, take the new medication, and when her cancer was gone and her numbers were good, she would go for the bone marrow transplant again. Only a few days before she was again scheduled to go into the hospital for the transplant, she became sick with an infection.

She was in the hospital for nine days when the family was notified that the infection had spread, and they were unsure whether or not they were going to be able to get it under control. Ultimately, her organs began to shut down, and her vitals became unstable.

Our kind Lizzie was surrounded by twenty family members praying and holding hands when she peacefully passed.

Lizzie's showed her kindness towards her family in so many ways. She was determined to stay for eight months and endure those painful procedures. She chose to deal with the uncertainty of her situation, knowing that she probably wouldn't be able to see her son grow up. She did it all to help her family deal with the situation.

Lizzie had helped to raise her nieces and had made many sacrifices to do that. She was dedicated to children and worked as a therapist for children with special needs. During one of her times at home, rather than just focusing on herself, she chose to go visit one of her "little boys" because she didn't want his parents to bring him into the hospital and have that memory of seeing her in there.

Lizzie was positive and filled with kindness throughout this whole ordeal. I personally have learned precious lessons about knowing your purpose, treating others with kindness, and making moments count. The strongest lesson was about having a positive attitude regardless of what you think the outcome may be.

None of us knows when our time will come. I believe that we all serve a specific purpose in this world. Lizzie served hers. Her life was filled with love for family, kindness, service to others, and confidence that she could help the rest of us deal with what was coming during her eight-month ordeal. I have been so touched by the acts of kindness surrounding this event. Our family circle has grown to include people that I didn't know before. Yes, we were brought together by tragedy, but we will be kept together by love.

Recently, I attended a yoga retreat up in the beautiful California mountains. The owner of the place where we stayed allowed us to plant a tree to commemorate our yoga retreat. I was given a few minutes to say a few words, which I dedicated to Lizzie. Shortly after that, a beautiful monarch butterfly was circling the tree and then me. I believe that the universe, the people in it, and our loved ones who have gone before us have all shared small and large moments of kindness.

We have this beautiful baby as a reminder of the kindness that Lizzie was all about and a determination to help Ryan in any way necessary to provide a beautiful life for Nathan. Ultimately, that's what Lizzie would do!

GINA MCELROY is a retired school teacher. She has 700 hours of yoga teaching certification hours and belongs to Yoga Alliance. Gina has her own yoga business, specializing in creating healthy bodies for her private clients. She enjoys teaching yoga to all ages, including children. She is Involved in the Mindfulness First organization that works to bring yoga and mindfulness into schools to aid with trauma. Gina is a certified mindfulness and guided imagery facilitator working with adults in and out of her yoga classes.

Gina co-authored the international best-selling book, *52 Weeks of Gratitude Journal* this past year and is so excited to be part of this *Kindness Crusader* book.

Connect with Gina
Facebook: gina.mcelroy.547

Week 39

What we all have in common is an appreciation

of kindness and compassion; all the religions

have this. We all lean towards love.

~ Richard Gere

THE GIFT OF RECEIVING KINDNESS

Most of you reading these stories are already nice, compassionate, and kind to everyone. The lesson here for you is to be kind and loving to yourself as well!

Take a calendar for the month and remember to mark your name on one or two days a week. So, when someone asks you for a favor, your eyes will see that time is already full and you won't give your time away. Later when you are going through your day suddenly you come to a time in the day that is just for you. Enjoy!

One day, Spirit told me to tell all the givers that they are unbalancing the world.

I asked, "Are you sure it's not the takers?"

Spirit said that until you love, honor, and are kind to yourself the way you are kind, loving, and giving to everyone else, there is a total imbalance. A taker cannot take unless a giver gives.

I answered, "I stand corrected."

It is important to ask within yourself to know when to help and be giving to others before you say yes and just do it. This way everyone wins. It's important to know when to be kind and giving out and when to be honoring the Light within you. It is a universal kindness.

I ask, "Spirit or God, is it my time to give?"

If I get a yes, I happily do it, but if I get a no then I say, "I am sorry I can't do that today." You don't even have to tell them why. Just give them truth with love from your beautiful heart. If we don't learn this lesson about when it is our time to do things for others, no one will ever learn the lesson of the dance of life. This is the way a taker can also learn the dance of giving and receiving through the kindness of truth with love. When you open your heart up to receiving kindness you will then be open to getting kindness given back to you. It's all about what you are letting into your life.

Look around at how many nice things happened and were given to you today. If you aren't receiving any or very little kindness, then you are blocking it from yourself. If you're receiving some kindness you can open to more.

During the holidays at my store, I always gave a larger love discount than my everyday one to help everyone with their gift shopping. A beautiful, kind, and generous lady had received a one-hundred-dollar discount on her purchases and gave the discount back to me. I became very uncomfortable.

After she left, I asked Spirit why this bothered me. I heard that I was okay with everyone loving and supporting the store, but anything above and beyond that felt selfish and greedy to me. I thought for a second and I realized that was true. I knew that I had to be kind and open to myself in order to receive more. That was my lesson. In that moment, I realized that I had to be open to receiving something big.

I asked what can I be open to that Spirit can give me that is big? Then I remembered that my husband said that it would be nice to have a place up north, so we could get away from the hectic life in Phoenix. I said I would like to have a place up north out in the country with nature so my husband can relax from his daily life. As soon as the thought traveled out of my mind, I immediately felt guilty. I already had a beautiful house and an amazing store that was kindly gifted to me by two wonderful new friends who graciously paid for everything for more than four years. Why would I need something more? I then said to myself that it was okay if the house was a fixer upper.

As soon as I said that I heard, "Judith, think big, think big, think big!"

I added, "Okay, with a stream."

I didn't say *on my property*, but the only way in or out of the complex is over a stream. When we went to the property there was a young deer grazing on the road next to the house.

I asked, "The deer is good, but is this my house?"

The deer stopped grazing, came over to where we were standing, jumped over the fence less than ten feet away, looked right at me, went to the back of the property, came back, looked again directly at me, and then jumped over the fence.

I said, "Okay God, the deer is good, but is this my sign to buy this property?"

Then a bluebird flew right over my head. In that moment, I started to cry happy tears. The realtor knew I was going to take the house before we even went inside. Guess what kind of house it was? Yes, a total fixer upper. LOL!

I then said, "Spirit, I learn fast. I realized you told me to think big, but I limited myself in my receiving kindness from the Universe. Now I know I could have asked for anything, and I settled on the limitations I created. Now I know whatever I choose to do to this house, Spirit, you will create it."

Whenever I had to buy something if it made my heart sing, I never even asked the price we would just buy it. I am shocked to this day that my husband went along with all my choices. Now it is a beautiful home doubled in size. This is what can happen to you if you are open to the kindness and gifts from Spirit for yourself. I always say now that *I choose this or better*. This way I am showing Spirit that I am open to receiving and that Spirit already knows what is best for me.

Now I am blessed with such a compassionate example of having someone showing me lots of kindness in my life. It's my wonderful husband Lou who makes me all my meals. In the past I used to make all our meals. The only time I make a meal now is when he is not at home. Since we are both 'sort of' retired that is not very often.

Kindness is also when all the people I knew would come to my store, A Peace of the Universe in Scottsdale, Arizona, whenever I had a book signing, a class, or events that I was participating in. I truly enjoyed when they would drop by for a visit for no reason at all. I love seeing my beautiful soul family members from my old store, which I was blessed to have for twenty-four amazing years.

As far as receiving kindness from others, I am pleased and grateful to say I am learning and finally embracing the lesson. I am thankful for all my beautiful teachers in my life who are teaching me and have already taught me the dance. I am still learning but happy to say I am way better at receiving the lesson of kindness.

JUDITH MANGANIELLO a New Jersey native, founded A Peace of the Universe Spiritual Bookstore in Scottsdale, Arizona. Judith is an author, teacher, an open channel with Spirit and the Angelic realm since childhood, numerologist, transformational healer, ordained minister, Reiki Master, and spiritual advisor.

Judith uses energy elevation, transferring negative thought-energy into positive results. People who have been fortunate to meet her know that she offers the most powerful, healing, and loving hugs.

Judith is the author of *A Giver's Way Home, Journey for Self-Love,* email Judith to receive your personal autographed copy.

Connect with Judith
Website: JudithAndSpirit.com
Email: judith999apotu@gmail.com
Phone: 480-338-9815

Week 40

Kindness is more than deeds. It is an attitude, an expression, a look, a touch. It is anything that lifts another person.

~ Plato

ORDINARY, EVERYDAY ACTS OF KINDNESS

Sometimes, even with the best of intentions, "life" gets in the way. We have a family cottage in Canada. A limb of a huge tree crashed down, hitting the side of our neighbor's house. It is located six hours away, and we haven't been there for ages due to my husband's health issues. But we needed to go immediately.

As we drove up, we discussed the need to sell this wonderful place, filled with 110 years of family memories. One family member had been using it sporadically for the past two years. He now lived about ten hours away and it was unlikely that he could care for it at all. We met with a realtor and put it up for sale. The work of clearing and cleaning began. Many treasures that served the family well over the years were worn and cracked. Physical things needed to be discarded, but the memories of all who spent their summers there are stored forever. This was to be my husband's last trip up there and he had to say goodbye. It was a hard and grief-stricken three days for him. He had been born right there in the living room seventy-nine years before.

Where does the kindness show up in the story? I was able to offer him the kindness of just being there. He needed to relive the memories and to grieve the passing of his summer home. I took care of all the details that are part of selling a property. We drove back home with heavy hearts, but we were filled with the sure knowledge that the time was right to offer this place to the next family to make their memories there.

The cottage sold in three days. The angels were definitely helping! My stepdaughter and I went back the next week and worked on packing, sorting, dumping contents, and saving the mementos. Her acts of kindness were very appreciated. She worked tirelessly to get as much done as possible in the three days that she had off work. She exemplified kindness in attitude and in deed.

Now that I have started writing again, many kindnesses come to mind.

My friend is ninety-five years old. She is quite independent, making her own doctors' appointments, taking great care of her medications. She lives alone in a senior apartment building where they put an "I'm okay" door hanger on their doorknobs when they rise in the morning. There is also one that says, "I'm away for the day."

As she makes various appointments, she calls me to make sure that I can pick her up and take her on that date. We always stop at the drive-through for drinks; hers is hot chocolate, and mine is coffee. If the time is right, we each have a sandwich for lunch. She asks to go to the drive-through so that she doesn't have to use her bothersome walker to get into a sit-down restaurant. Her kindness to me is that I don't have to wrestle that in and out an extra time. She is bright and cheerful, a real delight to be around.

The kindness in this story is twofold. First is her kindness to allow me the privilege of escorting her around town. I truly love this woman and enjoy our outings. She never complains. She lifts my spirit and gives me hope that a long and active life is possible. The second kindness is on my part. I carefully watch over her walking and only offer a helping hand when she asks for it. She walks, rolling her walker out of the apartment building, down to the car. I open the door as it is heavy for her. She backs in and hands off the walker. I take it around and stow it in the back of my SUV. By the time I get this accomplished, she is settled in the car and allows me to shut the door. And we are on our way.

Another kindness story is about my husband's actions when our elderly neighbor was very ill and spent most of the winter months in a hospital or nursing home for rehab. His wife spent each day with him. She left early in the morning and returned after dark. Each day my husband would take their paper and mail into their front porch. That way she didn't have to walk out to the street in the dark, cold night. This was a beautiful act of kindness as walking on ice and snow is very difficult for him.

In 2014 I was diagnosed with stage-three-B colon cancer. I was blessed to have hundreds of caring cards sent to me. It was a beautiful experience to open the mail each day to the many cards. Each one is treasured. The kindness of some who hardly know me except through a friend of a friend is still overwhelming. These people took time out of their busy days to send me prayers, greetings, and hugs! Oh, how precious are those cards. The cancer (now stage-four) came back in 2015 and 2016 and 2017 and people still rallied around me offering kind support and lifted me up on those dark days that are inevitable during several sessions of chemotherapy and radiation. I have now had two years of clear and clean scans. I try to pay it forward, offering kindness, love, and support where I can.

What does kindness mean to me? What does kindness mean to you?

♥ For me, it is always trying to walk in another's shoes to offer understanding and be non-judgmental.

♥ It is the simple attitude of making sure an elderly friend can maintain her sense of independence and dignity when and where she can.

♥ It certainly is shown by the hundreds of cards, prayers, thoughts, energy, and meals sent to me over the past few years as I was fighting colon cancer.

♥ And recently, it is the simple, no-strings-attached offer from my stepdaughter to help clear and clean the family cottage even though she has not been there for more than thirty years.

MARION ANDREWS is a bestselling author that strives to impart the knowledge and wisdom she has gained through many classes, certifications, and volunteer leadership positions. In a three-year fight against stage-four colon cancer, Marion discovered reiki as the way to healing your inner self as well as helping with your physical self.

Marion can offer you: relaxing, restorative reiki, in person or distant energy work, meditation, and online classes.

If you are ready to take a clear look at your life, no holds barred, book some life coaching sessions.

Schedule a fifteen-minute, free, video call by emailing or messaging Marion.

Connect with Marion
Website: chrysaliswellnesscenter.com
Email: marion@marionandrews.com
Facebook: ChrysalisWellnessCenter
Phone: 585-495-2435

Week 41

Your acts of kindness are iridescent wings of divine love, which linger and continue to uplift others long after your sharing.

~ Rumi

THE GIFTS OF KINDNESS

Within my work as a psychic medium and energy healer, I have learned a lot about kindness. I've learned how kindness shows up in people's lives unexpectedly from one person to another, and how it's given onto oneself or even inspired from a spontaneous source. Kindness as a gift comes in many forms.

Beautifully enough, there is opportunity for kindness, generosity, and a little something more each day. It all happens with a choice by yourself or another. Sometimes we find ourselves led on this path to kindness. Other times we have to be the ones that create the way. What vibration do you hold sacred? Is it kindness? What choices do you make in your own life to cultivate, experience, and return back to your sacred vibration regardless of where your corporal journey takes you?

When in a state of health, we do helpful activities for our condition of being each day, making intentional choices to nourish ourselves and sometimes even protecting what is dear to us. Early in my healing work, I began to spend more time with people of differing ages and backgrounds. I started to understand how important it was to create a bastion of what I held sacred for myself. And this revelation did not come necessarily from the things I was succeeding in, rather from the areas I was struggling with and what I sought to maintain and expand. This reflection came from areas of self-confidence, depression and sadness; questions of self-worth because my career was not where I wanted it to be; constantly having to reach out to businesses to create events or to see who was hiring; working hard and producing quality only to wonder what my bookings would be like in the next couple of weeks. There were high emotions in working so hard and having so little to show for consistently. There was a conflicting feeling from repeatedly having to show up and lay down new foundations rather than solidifying additions and moving upward.

At that time, in parallel, I was meeting people via my healing work who were going through depression, sadness and self-confidence lessons as well. Some were due to different reasons and others similar to my own. When I stepped into work, I'd shake off my circumstance, listen and be present with why the client had come that day. Reviewing their energy, during or after their healing session, I found myself being an advocate for them finding a way to their own understanding. My words and own energy moved to encourage them to the knowledge of clarity and achievable illumination.

The center factor being that I wanted them to see that they did not have to continue to suffer the same way within their circumstance; it was possible to find some semblance of what was next. It showed them that another option was waiting for them to be pursued, that there was something meaningful and flowing. It was an invitation for flexibility in understanding who and what they were capable of, all while healing and learning. To clarify, this reminder to thrive in life occurred on subconscious levels through sessions in reiki and chakra balancing, within readings, or during a coaching session. The healing sessions were all different, but they all held the same principles. Having lucidity to transmute pain or blockages does not have to be a gut-wrenching revelation even when we are smack dab in the trenches of our tribulations. It can simply be a surrender and allowance. When we look at ourselves and feel that something needs to change, and allow it to happen, not only is such an act of kindness, it's a conception of healing. Kindness is a grace and by being open to where it takes us, we receive its gifts.

Kindness led the way with me. The more I started observing client's energy and having conversations with them about it, I naturally began observing my own trials and tribulations with a kinder lens. I changed the way I met many of my repetitive conflicts with work and another chapter of my healing journey surfaced; my energy expanded. In actively using compassion in my readings and healings, I became undoubtedly kinder to myself. I simply couldn't separate or justify doing anything else because the people I was working with deserved nothing less. I established this understanding and therefore became devoted to viewing myself as a friend, family member, and loved one to my own self. A saying that I like to cultivate is that we can be "angels unto ourselves." The importance in this is we are all connected; there is absolute overlap in who we are, what we do, and the people we come across. Being kind onto ourselves contributes to healing the future cycles of many people we have yet to meet, share our time with, or even will help to nurture. We are a ripple effect, and, through this work, I wholeheartedly have seen what we do influences and matters. So, I'll throw it back in your court, toss you a question and say, "What is the kindest thing you have done for yourself today?"

KELLY BRICKEL is a certified master teacher of psychic and mediumship development through Lisa Williams' International School of Spiritual Development, certified Reiki Master teacher and certified master practitioner of NLP and MER®.

She works as a psychic-medium, healer, numerologist, mentor and spiritual coach. Kelly's passions are translating and working with Spirit as well as healing energy. She loves teaching and helping others find the beauty and strength of their gifts whether that be through becoming a reader, healer or more intuitive with their own lives. To schedule a reading, healing, or session contact Kelly by visiting her website.

Connect with Kelly
Website: energeticsessions.com
Instagram: Kelly Brickel

Week 42

Just imagine how different the world could be if we all spoke to everyone with respect and kindness.

~ Holly Branson

A COMMUNITY OF KINDNESS

It was a spring day in 2010 and I found myself on the scene of a horrific accident that had occurred in front of the store that I was managing. Sadly, four beautiful souls left this world that day, and five others had been critically injured. It was an event in my life that would spiral me into PTSD, but also one that would start me on my own journey to heal my past. It was a day that would not only alter the lives of many people and their families, but also changed a whole community.

The kindness and compassion that others showed after this experience was truly incredible. The following day we were honored with a visit from a police sergeant and a couple of the fire captains. These gentlemen went above and beyond their calls of duty when they stopped by the store to check in on myself and my employees to see how we were all doing. I will always be forever grateful to them, and the sergeant and his wife have become two of my best friends. The support that everyone in the community offered to us was truly unbelievable. People were coming in the store every day asking what they could do to help. They started donating money, and we put together a fundraising event to help those that were injured as well as the families of those that lost their lives. Every business owner in the area donated raffle items and food, and we were able to raise a large sum of money.

People seemed to be showing up from all over the country to pay their respects by hanging a bandana in the trees. They'd write a message or prayer on the cloth. There were over five hundred of those messages. I arrived at work one morning to find a Tibetan monk quietly standing under the bandana-filled trees. He began explaining to me the rituals and meaning behind the traditional Tibetan prayer flags. He told me how they are hung and that when the wind blows the prayers are sent up to the heavens. Right as he finished his story, a small breeze came and lifted all the bandanas up! I can still feel the chills that the movement sent through my whole body. The aunt of one of the ladies that lost her life found an inspiring way to honor the fallen four. She created handmade quilts from all the bandanas.

Those quilts were then given to all the families. One of my employees and I were also surprised with one of these very special gifts.

The memorial that was set up was huge. It was big as my kitchen and dining area. People filled it with balloons, flowers, pictures, posters, letters, cards, stuffed animals. One day after a terrible storm scattered lawn furniture all over my yard, I dreaded going to work because I knew that I would have to walk up and down the road gathering up all of the memorial mementos that people had left. When I arrived at the store, I could not believe what I saw, nothing at all had been disturbed or moved. It was like someone had placed a giant protective bubble over the whole thing.

A young man that had driven by after the accident wanted to create a memorial, so he donated his time and materials to build a beautiful permanent tribute that will always remain at the site. Within this metal sculpture is a stand in which a notebook is stored, People are still leaving messages inside. I know how much of an impact the kindness of others has had and what this has meant to the families as they will still go to the memorial and read the messages. It has helped them a little in their healing process.

There were groups of twenty to fifty bikers that would constantly stop by to pay their respects and ask what they could do to help. People came from out of state, and even a few from out of the country, just to honor the fallen. It was overwhelming, and amazing at the same time to watch people come together in such a time of need. The little acts of kindness, the thoughts, prayers, and support of everyone was just incredible to see, and I know how much it helped the families. It is impossible to share all of the amazing experiences of support that I was able to witness and share with the families. It truly made difference for them.

I was also fortunate to witness a very special act of kindness from a woman who had died in this tragedy. She had made the choice to be an organ donor. It was an incredible blessing to have met the recipient of her heart. She gave her the gift of life.

Never underestimate the power of kindness, no matter how big or small it might be. Your kind words and acts of service may truly have a life changing impact on someone. We don't have to wait for a terrible tragedy to show our compassion and kindness towards others, we can start today! Right now! Offer a smile to every person you meet. Tell the woman in the line at the store she looks pretty today. Thank a veteran, police officer or first responder for their service. Call someone out of the blue just to say hello. What can you do tomorrow to start your own kindness practice?

JANICE STORY brings over thirty years of expert horsemanship into her work as an equine coach. She is also a gifted certified Reiki Master/teacher, mind, body, and spirit practitioner, and a published author and speaker.

Janice's compassionate and gentle spirit provides safety for others. She has a strong connection with her team of seven horses who have always been a big part of her own healing. With the presence and unspoken language of her horses, together they are able to help create an opening for healing and transformation to occur in ways beyond that of human contact alone.

Connect with Janice
Website: janicestory.com
Email; janice.story@me.com

Week 43

Kindness boggles my mind. It's the only force

in nature that increases simultaneously

for the giver and the receiver.

~ Daniel Lubetzky

KINDNESS FOR THE SOUL

I always try to leave people a little better than how they were when I found them. Just listening as they tell you about their dreams, hardships, goals and fears is one of the kindest things you can do for people. They will remember your time and caring. It's a priceless moment that you have shared with them, and this puts them at ease to be their true and authentic selves. Sometimes just sitting beside them, holding their hands, or giving a simple hug is all someone might need at that moment.

At work one day, I had to help up front and be a cashier. One lady was my last customer before lunch. She had four small children. One was a baby. This woman was being unkind and nasty with her kids.

I stopped and really looked at her. Other customers were staring at her, and she was well on her way to a breakdown.

She laid her hand down on the counter and I took the opportunity to lay my hand and on top of hers.

I asked her if she was okay.

This beautiful young mother looked at me and said she just lost her husband in a car crash. She told me that she didn't know what to do.

My heart sank.

I immediately went around the other side of the counter and hugged her. It seemed like hours. It was only minutes. She sobbed and told me all about what happened. I cried too. I don't think there was a dry eye anywhere in the building.

I didn't let her go until I knew she was going to be okay to drive. I held the baby for a bit, hugged all the kids, and told her that I knew right now it felt like their world was crumbling but everything would be okay. I also told her that she could come see me at work anytime she needed a hug or someone to listen to her. I gave her my number.

A few weeks later she came in for a hug. She told me that what I did for her that day was the kindest thing anyone has ever done for her.

What she didn't know was that my heart grew a bit bigger that day. I knew that I had been right where I was meant to be for her.

Kindness is really a reciprocal thing. It's for the giver and the receiver. It's so easy for me to give kindness to someone else. I have a big heart and I like to share what I have learned about how to be happier in life. I find myself doing so much for others and forget about myself and being kind to me.

When you look at yourself and how much kindness you give to other people, you can just imagine giving some of that kindness to yourself and how amazing you would feel. One thing people can do for themselves every day is to just look in the mirror and say, "I love you. You are enough just the way you are. I'm proud of all the personal growth you have allowed into your soul. You are beautiful."

I know sometimes we don't always like our reflections in the mirror, but just remember we need to be right where we are right at this moment. There is something we need to learn from right now. We may not know what that is until days or years down the road. When we are kind to ourselves and really know how fabulous it feels to receive kindness, we truly can give kindness from our souls to others.

Take a few minutes each morning and sit quietly and meditate with deep breathing and letting go of all that no longer deserves you. Tell the universe that you are ready to receive all that you need. Then all the magic will happen.

I am a creative person who loves to make one-of-kind cards and give them to people who inspire me or just need a little sunshine in their days. I also sell my cards in store here in Okotoks, Alberta. Here is a quote from one of my customers who buys from me regularly.

"Dawn, you don't know me, but I thought that I should let you know that I often buy your handmade cards from Market on Main in Okotoks to send to my clients and friends. I thought that I should take a moment to let you know that everyone who receives your cards are so appreciative and love them so much. Thank you so much for producing such a beautiful product."

I'm forever grateful for my customers who love getting my cards as much as I love making them. When you are open to truly receive kindness into your heart and know how it feels, you can give to others to make their day a little bit better and your life will be blessed!

DAWN SLAMKO is a proud mother of two awesome children. She's been married for twenty-seven years and is the grandmother of a phenomenal special-needs grandson. She owns a home-based business making one-of-a-kind personal cards for all occasions. She has been based in or around Calgary, Alberta for most of her life and now resides in Okotoks Alberta.

The last number of years she has been reacquainted with her spiritual side and has really enjoyed studying the universe and what being grateful can do for people as they move forward during challenging times. This has led her to discover that when you are grateful and have an open heart then there are no boundaries at what someone can do.

Connect with Dawn
Email: dmslamko@hotmail.com
Face book: Dawn's Unique Creations

Week 44

Let no one ever come to you without leaving better and happier. Be the living expression of God's kindness in your face, kindness in your eyes, kindness in your smile.

~Mother Teresa

HOW KINDNESS INSPIRED MY CHARITY

It was December of 2012. I was healing after a walk-through stage-three peritoneal cancer. I was ready and willing to go back to my job and my work. I was grateful for a second chance at life. I was filled with the Holy Spirit and the Grace of God.

It wasn't enough.

We humans often value ourselves by our titles. I loved my job and telling people what I was. I was a health information management professional, a chart coder. I was one of the best, and I loved medicine and the responsibility I had. I loved working in a hospital.

Eventually, my employer felt it in their best interest to put me under a performance review for nine months. My attendance, performance, quality, and quota were being monitored. At the end of the nine months, they wouldn't release me from the terms of the review and so with my union's support we went to mediation.

Going up against a major employer in the province of Alberta is no easy task. Even though there were human rights violations in question, I was not a fighter. I knew that reducing my stress would be a major factor in my healing.

God guided me to leave my job of thirty-two years. Although I knew it was for my highest good, I was very sad. After my separation from my employment, I didn't know who I was. I felt guided to turn my focus to my love of all things divine.

Like the Mother Teresa guidance above, I asked God to allow me to be of service. I asked God to allow others to see God through me.

I disconnected from my job in 2016, but in 2015 I had already created Kindness Crew Calgary Society Ltd.

In the angel world, we have a saying, "When you get nervous, focus on service." It is so very true. I focused on being of service to my family, friends, city, province, country, world, and God.

You see, our souls just want to joyfully serve and stay in a constant state of joy and bliss. We are taught to get into the flow of giving and being open to receive. I'd felt so insecure when I was unsure about my future. However, the law of attraction helps us though. When we feel insecure, we can focus on being of service and then we receive all we need and more. And I did! I received money, opportunities, experiences, and teachers to help me propel my life to one I had only dreamed of.

I am happy, healing, and being of service. I am leading a wonderful group of souls that are Kindness Crew Calgary Society Ltd. And we love to give. We are a group of volunteers whose mission is to provide a hand up to the homeless population in Calgary. We are a small charity that does *big* work.

We have donated hundreds of blessing bags, which contain toiletries and personal hygiene items such as shampoo, conditioner, soap, body wash, shavers, combs and more. We also donate hundreds of pairs of socks, blankets, and towels. In the winter, we also provide gloves, toques and scarves so that people stay warm.

We are kindness in action. Kindness is an extension of love. Love is the highest healing quality. So not only am *I* healing, but we are healing our homeless with random acts of kindness.

Kindness is free. Sprinkle it everywhere!

GIULIANA MELO is a spiritual teacher, international bestselling author, and angel intuitive.

Giuliana is an inspirational speaker who has healed from cancer and now shares her story. She recently retired from thirty-two years in healthcare. She has been married for thirty-two years and has a twenty-one-year-old son.
To find out more or to help us, please contact Giuliana Melo.

Connect with Giuliana
Website: giulianamelo.com
Email: jmelo10@shaw.ca
Facebook: healwithgiulianamelo
Twitter: Jmelo10Julie

Week 45

Without kindness there can be no true joy.

~ Thomas Carlyle

ACTS OF KINDNESS LEAD TO ...

Kindness in all areas in our life is essential to experience true joy. That includes kindness to our self, significant other, parents, children, friends, and strangers. When one exhibits kindness to herself and others, it creates a feeling of joy for all the people involved. So why wouldn't we want our lives to be focused on kindness so that we can live in true joy on a more continual basis?

In *The Book of Joy*, the Dalai Lama and Desmond Tutu discuss how acts of kindness and compassion can cultivate a feeling of joy. Both of them wrote, "We are most joyful when we focus on others, not on ourselves. In short, bringing joy to others is the fastest way to experience joy in oneself."

When we pay attention to what is happening around us, we can see many acts of kindness whether they are random or planned. Each act of kindness fills the soul with joy to both the giver and receiver. If you have ever been on either end of kindness, then you know what I am talking about. It's that feeling of your heart wanting to jump out of your skin, a smile that goes from ear to ear, or chills running through your body.

Here are a few examples of some acts of kindness that have created intense joy to everyone involved.

Every Christmas season we do activities beginning on December 1 and ending December 24. Some are fun experiences; some are kindness activities. One of our acts of kindness is to write a note to our mail delivery person thanking him for all his hard work and long hours over the holiday season. Last year, we included a $5 Starbucks gift card. One night, my kids were waiting anxiously for him to come to our mailbox. When they saw the mail truck coming they ran outside in excitement and handed him the card. They came back a little unexcited.

I asked, "How did it go?"

They said, "It went fine, and he didn't say much."

The next night when we gathered our mail there was a random card. We opened it and it had two big, handwritten words on it, "Thank You."

The card said inside, "Of all the cards and tips this holiday season, I think yours is the kindest and nicest. Happy Holidays to you and your family."

Being on the giving end filled our hearts up with so much joy. Our children were jumping up and down with excitement. It filled my heart to see our children so excited about bringing joy and happiness to someone else's world.

On a cold winter day, my kids and I decided to go to the bowling alley. Initially we were the only ones there. As time went by, other people started to show up. After our second game, I went to pay.

The gentleman said, "Were you on lane five?"

When I told him that we were, he replied, "Someone already paid for your games."

Astonished I said, "What? Who?"

He pointed to the gentleman who was a couple lanes down from us and told me his name was Matt. I walked over to him in a state of disbelief and thanked him generously placing my hand on his arm.

He said, "My pleasure. It's so nice to see young kids enjoying a dying sport."

I turned and walked away bewildered, smiling, and my body filling up with one of the deepest sensations of joy I had ever felt. The kindness that man showed was tremendous! If I was to bet, then Matt probably felt joy as he paid it forward. I can't help but wonder how this situation even occurred for me as this is the first time someone has paid it forward to me.

When I shared this story with one of my friends, she said, "My friend, he did that because you already give so much to others."

These events and my short conversation with my friend caused me to explore other avenues of kindness.

When talking to a different friend about kindness, she said, "Kindness is when friends pick up the phone to talk to me when I'm going through a hard time."

I think of the times this friend had called me at 6:45 in the morning or after 10:00 at night. There were times I would say to myself, "I'll call her back." But then something compelled me to pick up the phone and I am always glad I did. It was those times she needed to talk to someone. At the end of our conversations, I can not only hear the gratitude she has but the joy it also brings her to talk to someone when needed.

We all have rough days and people around us catch on quickly that we're having struggles. Here are some examples of our children picking up on my rough patches and exhibiting kindness. I'll find my pajamas laid out on my bed and a book by my pillow. Dishes are washed and put away. The kitchen island is completely cleared off. The best acts of kindness by far are the extra hugs, kisses, and cuddles I get from our children. Each of us has a choice in creating the opportunity to create joy in another's heart through being kind or not. If we choose to be kind then we make an immediate difference in others' lives. These examples show how kindness and joy go hand in hand. The more kindness we exhibit and accept the more joy we will feel in our lives.

Imagine doing one act of kindness a day and having one more moment of joy in your world. Do you think you will be happier and more joyful? You bet you will!

Each morning when you wake up, set two intentions. Number one: Do one act of kindness today to someone else. Number two: Receive an act of kindness today. Put the intention out there and move on. Keep your eyes open, be present in the moment throughout the entire day.

Listen when that little voice in your head says, "Hold the door for that person." Listen when it tells you to give your child an extra hug and kiss and do it without even thinking twice. Take note of how that other person reacts, the joy-energy that exerts from them, and the feeling of joy that fills you up. No matter how big or small, when you are engaged in any kind of act of kindness, you will know when it happens. Once you become aware of these acts, you can start changing your patterns and behaviors to create more kindness in the world and joy in your life.

LAUREN ALEZA RAYMOND is an elementary educator and founder of Daily Joy LLC where she privately coaches parents to build JOYFUL homes where everyone feels loved, heard, and nurtured so that a house can truly be a sanctuary of peace. Her program is based on creating joy in three areas: self, relationships, and parenting. Together this creates joyful homes.

Together, let's build you a joyful home where everyone feels loved, heard, and nurtured so that your house can truly be a sanctuary of peace. Mention that you saw this in the book Kindness Crusader and receive 25 percent off one-on-one coaching.

Connect with Lauren
Website: dailyjoy.us
Email: lauren@dailyjoy.us
Facebook: laurensdailyjoy
Instagram: laurensdailyjoy

Week 46

Deliberately seek opportunities for kindness, sympathy, and patience.

~ Evelyn Underhill

A DIVINE GIFT OF KINDNESS

For most people an act of kindness just comes naturally. You open a door for someone, offer a smile, a soft touch, a kind word, or pay for someone's lunch. You may never know the impact that you have had on that person's day or even their life.

Sometimes you are on the receiving end of the same kindness that you offer others.

I had been through so much loss. In just a few years, I'd lost my husband, mother, sister, and brother, which was basically my whole support team. I was spending most of my time taking self-help courses, studying with excellent teachers and mentors. I joined support groups, basically working on healing my mind, body and spirit, trying to find myself. I was on a healing journey.

Growing and healing, I felt proud of the progress that I was making. I had been asking for answers as to where my new path should take me. I wanted to know what I should do with my sixty-five years of life experiences. The answer to my prayers came to me at the most unexpected time.

I was having one of those weeks where I felt like I could not go on. I could not settle myself down no matter how hard I tried. It all started as I was brushing my little fur baby. I came across a tick that had obviously been on him for a couple of days. I was totally mortified. I had never seen anything so disgusting in my life.

As I examined him further, I found some fleas. Normally, I would have just put on some spray and a collar and continued with my life. Instead, I went into a complete crisis mode. The tick frightened me because of diseases that ticks may carry. Ill from the thought of having ticks or fleas on my fur baby or in my home, I could not figure out where they had come from. More importantly, I didn't know how I would get rid of them. I totally freaked out!

I started researching on how to get rid of them. The more I found out, the more frightened I became. I started aggressively treating my fur baby, my home, and myself. I was itchy, sick to my stomach. I could not even sleep. Every emotion started to surface: anger, fear, frustration, grief. I felt so overwhelmed. I was sure that I couldn't handle this by myself. I felt inadequate, not good enough. I had no support team, no one to talk to, help me, or even offer some me compassion.

Why was I even trying? What was my purpose anyway? I wondered.

After four days of this anxiety and negative self-talk, I needed to get out of the house and out of the chaos of my mind. I decided to call my daughter and meet her for lunch. That morning I took a shower, got dressed, and prepared myself for the day. Thanks to this self-care, I was already starting to feel some relief from the stress.

I decided to surrender and just go with the flow of the experience. I asked my angels for support and I drove off to meet my daughter. Just as I pulled into the parking lot, my daughter called and said she could not make it. Through all the confusion, I had misunderstood her plans for the day. I took a deep breath. Still somewhat distressed, I decided that a drive-thru lunch would be the best for me. On the corner I had three choices, Burger King, Arby's, or McDonald's.

Yes, fast food.

Yes, I'd be eating it in the car.

This would give me time to sit, unwind, and just be. I decided on Burger King because a chicken sandwich sounded okay. I drove into the lot. When I looked up, I realized that I was at Arby's. I had pulled into the wrong drive thru.

I ordered my roast beef sandwich through the speaker. The worker asked if I would like to upgrade to a meal. At this point, I just wanted something to eat, to be able to just sit and relax.

When I reached the window to pay, I was expecting to hear my total. Instead, I was pleasantly greeted by a beautiful and kind smile. The worker looked me in the eyes and explained that someone had bought my lunch today. But who? There was no one else in the parking lot behind me or ahead of me.

She proceeded to show me a picture of a gentleman and stated that this was Randy. He was a special-needs person that loved to have his lunch at Arby's. Every single time that Randy's mother brought him there, he would pay for his lunch, his mother's, and the lunch of the people in whatever car was behind him.

Randy had recently passed away. His wishes were for his mother to leave a gift card at Arby's. He could continue his acts of kindness.

My heart swelled. Tears started to flow and chills washed over me. I could not even express myself. I was so filled with gratitude, love, and compassion for Randy and his mother that I could not think of anything else. I just wanted to shout to the world about what an amazing blessing this gift of kindness was for me.

The clerk asked that I please say a few kind words for Randy that day.

Randy's act inspired me to tell his story and to continue to inspire others with love and kindness. It validated to me that when you surrender all obstacles and distractions to love and kindness, you will be guided to where you need to be. You are enough just as you are. You do not need a title, label, or a certificate to be kind. You will not find happiness outside of yourself. Most importantly, you will be remembered more for your kindness than for anything you could ever achieve. I will never forget the kind smile from the lady at the window, Randy's beautiful face in that picture, his golden heart, or his divine gift of kindness. Randy's love and kindness have truly changed my life. I now understand that my purpose in this world is to just be me, to inspire others and myself with love and kindness.

Just be you.

Just be brave.

Just be kind.

Just be true to yourself and others

ELISE SCHEMA is a kindness crusader, author, mentor, caretaker, mother, and grandmother. She was born and raised in Michigan. Her life passion is studying and practicing holistic healing of the mind, body, and spirit. She belongs to support groups and loves connecting with like-minded people. She loves inspiring others with her sixty-five years of life experiences and knowledge.

Elise is inspired by life's challenges, enjoying nature, traveling, and embracing life to its fullest.

She loves inspiring others by being the best version of herself, sharing love, joy, and kindness.

Connect with Elise
Facebook: Elise Grace Schema
Email: Eliseschema13@gmail.com

Week 47

We have to be active about kindness and about

peace. I've always fantasized that it would

be great if there was a Department of Peace.

~ Dave Matthews

YOU ARE WORTHY

For most of us, kindness is instinctual. We are born with an innate capacity to give, to serve, and to love with devoted kindness. As I look back over my life, I can see that being kind was effortless. It was something I believed in. I knew early on I wanted to heal and to be a warrior for the underprivileged, the hurting, the ones struggling to be heard and seen. I knew that kindness could transform a shattered life and a weary, adrift soul. There seems to me that there is no other way to live other than to give unselfishly and without judgement. Isn't it our duty to be kind to our fellow human beings? The answer is as simple as the act itself.

I have always felt part of my purpose was living to exemplify the creator and all He has taught us. When we can remember that we are all created to love and to be loved, kindness lives within us.

Several months ago, in the middle of many seemingly endless crises, I had a sudden realization. One may call it an a-ha moment or an eye opener. My marriage had been given the final curtain call. The man that I had known since childhood and that I had borne five children with had moved miles away. My nest of children began to fly far away to begin their lives. We were hit with some mental health challenges and severe depression. Unwelcomed changes seemed to be arriving daily to challenge our fractured family. In the midst of all this, maintaining faith and strength were paramount and yet sometimes undeniably difficult. The phrase 'one day at a time' took on new meaning. It became a mantra. Sometimes I said this to myself every hour, repeating it over and over, hoping that I could just simply stand one more minute. It was during these most trying of times that the power of kindness was most evident in my journey. It seemed that just when I could longer budge one more inch, I was shown an act of kindness. It was almost always unexpected and sometimes came from complete strangers. Despite immense pain and struggle, kindness was showing up dressed in beauty and grace. It was being given freely and unselfishly, offering my soul a life preserver.

As I was navigating this precarious road that I found myself on, I was finding hope in the kindness in others. My a-ha moment screamed to me. I was passing by my mirror in the hallway and caught a glimpse of myself. It seemed unreal to me and it almost took my breath away. The person staring back at me could not really be me! Had I really avoided looking at myself for so long that I could not recognize the woman staring back at me? Hollow eyes, dark circles and was that really all the hair I had left? Staring back at me was a sad, broken, stressed shell; she was a person who had never been kind to herself. She was the person who believed that you cannot live without kindness.

You must always give. You must always serve with love, and never let anyone do without or not feel loved. All this time, I have neglected the person in the mirror, a person also given life by the Creator just as everyone else was. She was a person also loved by the same Creator; why had I not loved myself? Why had I failed at being kind to myself?

We all don our capes. This is especially true for women. We make sure that everyone is cared for, and yet we put our needs aside like yesterday's trash. Our spouses, children, jobs, co-workers, friends, and family become the focus of our giving and in all of this we forget that we must be taken care of also. We must be willing to place our oxygen mask on first. We cannot quench another thirst until we quench our own or one day, we will be too dehydrated to give anything else.

I have spent countless hours reminding others how they must care for themselves, how they must value and honor themselves. Yet, I have never done this for myself. The woman staring back at me with pleading eyes reminded me that it was time. It was time to be kind to me. It was time to love me. Then and only then could I offer this gift to others.

I have been so grateful for the kindness of others in my life and I have taken great joy in giving, but I know now that I am also worthy to be kind to myself. I can serve others with a greater purpose and with my cup that is not running empty. I can now be a living example of what I teach to so many.

Take some time today to look in the mirror and really see what is staring back at you. Take a few moments to love that person as much as you would anyone else. Tell that person they are worthy to be loved and cared for. Be kind to you.

LORI GERAGHTY is an aspiring writer and a certified spiritual life coach. With her background in psychology, she takes her knowledge and experience and works primarily with women recovering from abusive relationships. She has a passion for women's mental health wellness and is a champion for mental health advocacy.

Lori is "Mama" to five amazing humans and loves writing, traveling, art, music and dance.

Connect with Lori
Email; lorianna923@gmail.com

Week 48

The way I stand up to bullies is with kindness and love. Because I think that's what they really need. They're misunderstood and probably really upset themselves.

~ Chrissy Metz

KILL THEM WITH KINDNESS

Kill them with kindness is a phrase often used when someone exhibits compassion and unwavering love in the face of anger and hate. Many people find it hard not to fight back when someone is being unkind or hateful. Revenge is often the first reaction. It has been described as *fighting fire with fire.* I love this analogy, if you fight *fire with fire* you are going to get burned. Anger and hate create more anger and hate, no matter how justified we may feel in the moment. Killing with kindness is to rise above the ego and stop anger and hate by responding with compassion and love. Here is my story of how unwavering kindness influenced healing for myself and others.

Mother Teresa and Gandhi were just two of my mother's heroes. She often shared stories of how they remained unconditionally kind even when faced with anger and hate. They both had the ability to rise above emotions, exhibit self-control, and show everyone that there is nothing in this world that could take away the love and kindness in their hearts. It was their strength of love from within that brought the greatest examples of kindness ever witnessed. They really knew how to *kill them with kindness,* and they went down in history for it. My hippie, activist mother was good at following their leads and encouraged me to do the same.

I started using this *kill them with kindness* mentality at an unusually young age. I remember being in elementary school and receiving negative attention from a boy who was poking fun and pushing me around. Instinctively, I responded with kindness by telling the kid that I just wanted to be friends. I will never forget the shocked look on this little boy's face when I showed him kindness instead of anger. Immediately the bullying stopped, and we did become friends.

This became my mode of operation whenever faced with anger and hatred from another. The influence of my mother anchored the belief that the antidote to anger is love. It is no surprise that my career path led me to a position of creating comfort in uncomfortable situations. My eighteen years of experience working in a dental office often required a kind response from me. I had to learn deep compassion for patients who were fearful of the dentist and angry about their bills. I was often given the task of helping angry patients because I am notoriously known for maintaining my kind composure.

Although I have always been known for being a kind person, my kindness was limited. For years, I could not see how I could possibly help others and make a difference in the world. That was because I did not understand my own value. I was living small and doing just enough to survive.

Despite the fact that my mom was a huge advocate for self-love and self-care, I ignored her advice to meditate, use positive affirmations, and breathe. I passed it off as woo-woo hippie stuff and allowed myself to be negatively influenced by a fast-paced lifestyle and challenging circumstances. I was kind to the people outside of my home. In my home? It was a different story. I would often explode in anger and frustration and blame my family for my unhappiness.

Depression slowly crept into my experience, but I didn't realize it until our county was devastated by the 2017 firestorms. The fires burned hundreds of homes and displaced thousands of people. I saw great kindness on the news as the community came together to donate items, raise money, and volunteer in shelters. I wanted to be one of the kind people helping, but instead I became almost paralyzed as depression set in deeper.

My home and family were safe, but we did take a hit financially. My partner's masonry business came to a halt. The current home he was working on burned down as well as the jobs he had lined up. On top of that, no one was eager to get going on a new project. My partner sat at home with no work for months. Financial hardship plagued my family while I comforted myself with cheap wine and food.

I found myself weighing more than ever before, fighting with my partner all the time, and unable to give my son the support he needed. I knew that no matter what was going on around me, I had to do something to just feel better. I began thinking about the things my mom had taught me about self-love and spiritual practice. They were the stable foundation that remained when all life structures failed. I saw that these foundations were missing in my life, and my structures were not stable. I finally took my mom's advice and started meditating.

Before any of my circumstances changed, I began to feel better. This meditation thing really worked. I felt inspired to make changes in my diet and develop a spiritual practice. *The Universe Has Your Back* by Gabrielle Bernstein fell into my lap. This book summed up everything my mom tried to teach me written in words I could relate to. For the first time, I felt connected to a higher power of my own understanding and began to realize that I am an important part of the universe. I saw that I was taking my unique gifts and talents for granted and that I must share them with the world in order to find happiness and success.

I heard a calling to be more kind to myself so that I could extend that kindness to others. In order to follow this calling, I needed to take better care of my body and gain the energy to follow my dreams. I received support from a wellness coach, did a cleanse, followed the ketogenic diet, and killed my pain with kindness. That means that I stopped the negative self-talk and started saying loving things to myself. I easily lost fifty pounds and gained clarity about my purpose in life, which was to help others heal through my example. My coach saw my desire to help others. She mentored me and I became a women's empowerment coach.

It has now been almost two years since the fires and all structures of my life are stronger than ever. I just recently became a mind-body medicine-skills practitioner, and I am now helping my community heal from the stress and trauma that many people suffered in the aftermath of the fires. The Sonoma Community Resilience Collaborative partnered with The Center for Mind-Body Medicine and raised 1.4 million dollars to provide a free training program to anyone who wanted to help heal the community. I was gifted this training and now am serving my community in a big way.

Clearly, I see that we must be kind to ourselves first so that we can fully show up for others. The greatest act of kindness is to know your own self-worth so you can kill anger, hate, pain, and sadness in the world with kindness through your own example of unconditional love for yourself and life.

Unwavering kindness starts from within.

HEATHER HANSON is a women's empowerment coach, motivational speaker, writer, singer, artist, and keto chef. She empowers women to transform their wellbeing and lifestyle by changing habits, nutrition, and mindset.

Through her own healing journey and authentic sharing, she inspires women to use evidence-based, mind-body medicine tools to raise their energetic vibration and unlock their full potentials. She offers healing workshops, online courses, and one-on-one coaching. She has a passion for creating enjoyable low-carbohydrate, low-sugar treats to help women balance their hormones, heal their guts, and lose weight without feeling deprived.

Connect with Heather
Website: heatherempowersyou.com

Week 49

I always say that kindness is the

greatest beauty that you can have.

~ Andie MacDowell

THE KINDLED LIFE

Mark was a nineteen-year-old, college undergrad attending one of the most sought-after universities in the country. Some friends, some family, some money, he had *some* of everything. Yet he could not feel *enough*, not enough of himself, not enough of his past, not enough of his future. Alienated from everything and everybody, his isolation grew bigger and bigger, until it became too big of a pain to handle. He was tired of feeling like the creepy guy everybody did not want around. He felt that despite all his attempts to be part of a group; he could not belong. His pain became unbearable, and one day while going to class he looked at his watch. He was thinking of how useless his life was when nothing meaningful could ever happened. He felt that his was most insignificant existence, which did not deserve even a round of the clock.

Mark stopped to sit on a campus bench. He got angry; his life was not even worth his own effort. He was different from most of his fellow students, which they constantly reminded him about. They said he was weird.

"And maybe they were right," he thought.

He made up his mind right that instant. He would not go to class, not that day, not the day after, not anymore. He thought that while he had no power to be as they wanted him to be, he did have the power to decide about his existence. He could do something. He could stop right there what he believed to be the insignificance of his life. The eerie guy would withdraw from the madness of this earthly presence. Nobody would anyway notice the oddball's absence.

Mark threw his books as far away as he could. His chest was pumping as if all his rage wanted to come out at once. He also had a sense of relief for the decision he had just made. He fought all those images that were playing in his mind as the movie of his childhood passed by, his mother, the rest of his family. He fought all that because he knew that stopping right there was the right decision.

It was a cold winter morning, thirty-one degrees.

He stood there for hours. He was so enthralled by his thoughts that he didn't suffer the cold or notice people passing by.

When his fingers were so cold that he couldn't feel them inside his gloves, he heard somebody shouting.

A young fellow was in Mark's face bellowing, "Hey you! These books? Are these books yours! Hey you! Hey you!"

The young guy kept yelling insistently and repeatedly about the books on the wet ground some yards away from the bench. As soon as he saw Mark blinking, he sat next to him and started to talk, "It is damn cold this morning and I had a rough week, you probably too? My mother is mad at me for failing my semester, she is saying, 'I am squandering my life … !' Maybe she's right, but I feel confused. I have no motivation to study. I do not even know whether this is what I want to study or what I want to do. My brother was all another story, always knew where he wanted to go. And listen to this, *how* he wanted to get there. My girlfriend dumped me. It's cold today man it's really cold! Are you cold? You should be cold; I'm freezing here …"

He continued ranting about his ex-girlfriend. He seemingly could care less about whether Mark was answering any of his questions or quiet, but he kept on sitting next to him.

The young man did not care much anyway about answers. He seemed restless. Mark wondered why he didn't just leave.

To Mark's surprise the young man said, "Hey, I am Simon and I am sure you are having a rough day too. Wanna come with me to shoot some hoops? My next class was cancelled anyway, and I am not taking *no* for answer."

Mark found his cheeky offer out of place, but for some reason while his mind wanted him to utter a no, his mouth said yes.

Mark stood up slowly, baffled, wondering why on earth he was even following Simon. His day ended up being a good one.

They played basketball together innumerable times. Simon showed up at Mark's doorstep many other times and a friendship was born. It was a friendship where Simon never asked Mark why he'd been sitting there in the cold, or why he had thrown away his books. For years, they have been there for each other's studies, life challenges, failures, and successes.

On Mark's graduation day, he was called up to the podium to give his speech.

He started by thanking life for giving him the beautiful gift of existence and the harsh opportunities to mould him into the man he had become. He expressed his gratitude for the wonderful opportunities he had in life but most of all for an amazing gift that he received some years prior in a cold morning when he was sitting on a bench: an invitation to play.

Should that amazing act of kindness not have happened he would have not been there, and he would have not been alive.

On the day when he decided to end his life and his pain forever, somebody collected his books from the slushy snowy ground and asked him to go to the basketball court. That moment, that invitation, that act of kindness was the turning point of his life.

He went from a life which was not worth of living to a life he loved living and where he thrived.

Simon applauded, barely holding back his tears. He could not have made it without Mark when he grieved his mother's passing and so many other times. Simon had lost his father by suicide and he had never known that Mark had ever thought of ending his life. Simon kept on clapping, overjoyed with the love he had for his friend, thinking that no matter what happened in their lives, they would have been there for each other forever.

ANTONELLA LO RE is the author of *Seven Steps to Joy*, a book where she reveals seven inner abilities that we all can tap into to navigate serenely the storms of life. Intuitive, witty, and enthusiastic about life, Antonella is a multilingual and international traveller who enjoys the role of writer and self-improver. Of Italian origin, she divides her time between the United States and Switzerland.

Her strongest wish: to be part of those who want to make a difference.

Her favourite things to do besides writing: take every day as an opportunity to evolve and grow up, not grow only older!

Connect with Antonella
Website: antonellalore.com

Week 50

Kindness and politeness are not overrated at all. They're underused.

~ Tommy Lee Jones

BEING KIND TO YOURSELF RIPPLES OUT TO OTHERS

There have been many times acts of kindness have flowed through my life. I realized after years of giving and receiving, that kind acts were not filling my soul. I couldn't understand why. I enjoyed giving and serving others. I felt something was missing in me.

Still, at times, I would feel resentment inside as I freely gave with love. I didn't know how this could be. I would ask the questions, *what is wrong with me? Why am I giving but feel drained?*

I felt depleted. I was giving, loving, and kind to others, and it was not being returned. I was feeling empty and frustrated. My thoughts were how I was giving kindness, and no one was returning it. This was the beginning of my journey back to myself and my understanding of real, loving acts of kindness. Now, that kindness is free-flowing and endless within me.

However, back then, I had to stop and ask myself, *Why? What was missing?* Being kind to others was always just a part of my thinking deep within my heart. What had changed? I always loved to give to others freely with no questions, no expectations.

I started to realize after asking myself why – after years of working on myself. Also, being the observer of life and my actions – that I 'didn't know how to be kind and loving to myself. As I unfolded the pieces of my life, I realized being unkind to myself was blocking the goodness of showing others a deeper kindness. I could see from the fruits within my life this was true. I was feeling depleted, frustrated, and most importantly? I was resentful.

I was not fulfilling my deep desires and not loving and respecting myself. I was giving to people but had an empty hole within me. I was giving freely to others but closed the door to receive it. When kindness was flowing to me, I would put a wall up and send it back. I would question people's motives. I am sure there were times I hadn't even notice when someone was kind because I was closed off. I was skeptical when someone was kind because of old stories and beliefs that were no longer true.

Could someone genuinely want to be kind? I wondered. To me?

From my experience, I am not alone in feeling this way. I was a full-fledged victim in my life. I'd decided this was going to change.

I believe kindness is a giving *and* a receiving action. Both are equally healing and needed for balance. My journey started when I dug deep to find what needed healing. I then saw more clearly who I was. I began to see the roots of my issue. I hated myself and was far from kind to myself. With much inner work, I began to see the truth. I replaced my old beliefs. I learned that everyone, including myself, deserves love and kindness, not everyone except myself.

I would love to ask you to stop and evaluate your relationship with yourself. Do you have a respectful and loving relationship with who you are?

I learned I could not freely give until I learned to love and be kind to me. I never stop giving and loving others. I willingly gave as I saw a need. I allow the energy to flow freely and unconditionally from new eyes. It is a joy to see so many new ways to give and help others. No matter how big or small, it always brings me peace and joy.

When we take steps toward healing ourselves from old beliefs, the whole world starts a healing process, bringing peace to the world. That is one of the biggest acts of kindness we can give. When we are kind to others with a full heart, it is pure and free. That's giving with no expectations back and no attachments.

As I walk down the street and give a big smile, say hello to a stranger, and they reject my gesture, I remember I don't know their story. I send them love and blessings for a beautiful day. That goodness and love will fill them and touch their hearts.

It is not about them accepting or rejecting my action. It helps to raise the vibration. It doesn't matter whether people know about it or not. They will still be affected by it.

Showing kindness to others can be interesting. I had been to the post office. This gentleman needed to buy a stamp. He only had a dollar bill, and the post office didn't have change. He was frustrated and angry. As I observed the situation, I calmly paid for his stamp. He was so shocked and embarrassed. He almost crawled out of his skin. He didn't know how to act. This was a small act but caused a big reaction in the post office. I was reminded about how one action could affect several people. I reassured him all was okay and to return the gift.

Being kind now flows through me effortlessly and with ease. It is merely a part of who I am. I don't question my actions any longer. It just is. Being kind brightens my soul. It lifts my vibration. It is the best thing to do when you are having a bad day. Go out and find someone to help. Try it. Understand that being kind and loving to others is the best road to healing ourselves.

If I am short, angry, or judgmental in my day, I know that it is time to realign my thinking. I am in my head and out of alignment with who I am. I need to make sure I am showing kindness toward myself, thinking kind words, and having compassionate acceptance and loving forgiveness and showing sweet patience. I have to remember to allow myself to enjoy being me. Giving myself time to rejuvenate and connecting to myself through meditation every day is vital for my balance. I now listen and trust my inner guidance. If you take the time to love and be kind to yourself, then ways to be kind to others will always be in front of you. It will flow through you with ease. I am free to love and give to others with no thoughts and have joy in my heart. If I am not, I need a reset.

Kindness is something that comes from deep within. It is given unconditionally, given in love, not an obligation.

JOANNE EISEN is a student, teacher, and mentor. According to JoAnne, "I have a gift of being a truth-sayer. I quickly shine a light on your truth of what you have forgotten hidden inside. I help locate your beautiful spark wanting to be expressed — your hidden treasures. I've spent years learning and healing my old stories. I share my knowledge and training to gift you with the tools to move forward."

You can check out her website and schedule a free discovery call or catch her weekly Facebook Live show and learn how others reach the next level in their lives on Facebook or YouTube.

Connect with Joanne
Website: reachtheunlimited.com
Email: joanne@reachtheunlimited.com
Facebook: reachtheunlimted
YouTube: JoAnne Eisen

Week 51

Kindness is a passport that opens doors and fashions friends. It softens hearts and molds relationships that can last lifetimes.

~ Joseph B. Wirthlin

KINDNESS KARMA

It was one of those hot summer days in Palm Springs, California where the overnight cool was ninety degrees. I knew that it would be busy at work with everyone wanting to be inside to beat the heat. Working as a makeup artist for a high-end cosmetic line gave me a lot of perks and being indoors during the summer months was one of them. My workday started like any other day with greeting customers, offering makeup tips, and makeovers. All makeup artists where I worked received an hourly wage plus commission on anything we might sell, and with a high-end cosmetic line that can be a very lucrative and attractive bonus.

Later in the afternoon, a couple of young ladies came into the store. I think the smell made me look up before I saw them. They seemed to be around fifteen or sixteen years old, wearing wrinkled and mismatched clothes. There was dirt on their faces, and it appeared as if it had been several days since a brush or comb had touched their hair. As they came up to my counter, I immediately noticed our plainclothes security guard standing discretely in the background as my fellow makeup artist began moving away from our guests.

"Hi, how can I help you?" I asked.

One of the young ladies responded, "I can't buy anything, I'm just looking really."

"Wonderful, what would you like to try today?"

As I was reaching into one of the drawers to pull out several samples, one of my coworkers tapped me on the shoulder, whispering in my ear, "You know these are street kids right, and they don't have any money."

"Yes, I know," I said and went back to my guests.

After that encounter, one of the young ladies left, but the other stayed. I asked her a little bit about what kind of makeup she liked and how she liked to look.

She answered, "A more natural look but heavy on the eyeliner and lip."

I offered her a full makeover and asked if she would like to sit in my chair.

"Yes, I would, but you know I can't buy anything," she said.

"We have a new makeup line I've been trying to practice with, and you'd be helping me out. I could really use a model."

She sat down and we started talking. I discovered that her name was Suzie and her friend's name was Jill. They were fourteen and fifteen and had been squatting with some other young people somewhere in the area. They had come into the store to get out of the heat because they didn't have air-conditioning where they were living. During Suzie's makeover, I cleansed her face, brushed her hair, and applied some natural makeup, heavy on the eyeliner and lip just like she wanted. I also found out that both young ladies had run away from their homes over a year ago. They'd lived somewhere on the East Coast.

While we talked and I worked on her make-up, I told her about a friend of mine who was a youth minister at one of the local churches. I mentioned that sometimes, when things got tough for people like her and Jill, he could help. I emphasized that they would keep their information confidential if that's what they wanted.

"It might come in handy to take his name and phone number. Will you do that?" I asked.

Suzie shrugged her shoulders. "I can take the number, I guess."

As she was getting ready to leave, I prepared a sample bag for her. It included face cleanser, a comb, and makeup samples. Unlike my regular sample bags, this one also contained my friend's phone number and twenty dollars. I sensed that it had been a while since Suzie and Jill had eaten anything.

When I handed her the bag she said, "I can't pay for that."

"It's my gift to you for being my model today, thank you. Please look in the bag before you leave the mall," I said.

The security guard was still standing at the front of the store, and I glared him down as she was leaving. He responded by shaking his head and walking away. I watched Suzie and Jill open the bag together and hug each other when they discovered the twenty dollars.

Suzie looked back at me and mouthed, "Thank you."

When I left worked that evening it was at least 120 degrees, the sun had already set, and it was still so hot that it took my breath away. I had to turn the car and air conditioning on and then get back out of the car until it reached a temperature I could tolerate. The traffic was terrible that evening. I decided to take the back roads home.

This was back in the day when reliable transportation meant the car ran most of the time, and there were no cell phones.

About halfway home, my car died in the middle of the road. It was dark, hot, and I was too scared to get out of my car and walk along an isolated desert highway. I didn't know what else to do, so I turned my emergency flashers on and prayed. About five minutes later, lights appeared in the middle of the rearview mirror. The car stopped right behind me. I was relieved and a little alarmed to see a lumberjack of a man come up to my window. I just rolled my window down a little.

"Thank you for stopping," I said.

It was like he read my mind and said, "No problem. Just pop the hood and I can look. No need to get out of the car. I have a younger sister and I wouldn't want her getting out of the car this time of night with a total stranger."

My unexpected hero got my car running for me again. He even gave me the prognosis for my car. That way I would know what to tell the mechanic.

"You'll be okay till you get home, but don't stop anywhere until then," he said.

I thanked him and was so grateful for the kindness of this stranger.

As I laid my head on the pillow later that night, I thought about the extraordinary day and how kindness comes in surprising and unexpected ways. I thought about Jill and Suzie and if they were safe. I prayed that they were, and that the kindness of strangers continued to wrap them in love and protection.

CAROLAN DICKINSON is a psychic medium, angel communicator, teacher, and author of her debut women's fiction novel, *Three Full Moons* (scheduled for release in late 2019). She is also the author of the bestsellers *52 Weeks of Gratitude Journal* (2018), *111-Morning Meditations-Start Your Day with Intention* (2017) and *Walking with the Archangels* (2015).

Her first love is doing private readings and helping people discover their own gifts and talents. She teaches intuitive and personal development classes both in person and online. In her free time, you will find her in a yoga class, reading, or walking and talking with the archangels.

To work with Carolan or follow her weekly archangel blog, please visit her website.

Connect with Carolan

Website: carolandickinson.com
Facebook: carolandickinson
Instagram: carolandickinson

Week 52

*Human kindness has never weakened the
stamina or softened the fiber of a free people.
A nation does not have to be cruel to be tough.*

~ Franklin D. Roosevelt

ISLAND FAMILY OPENS THEIR HEARTS & HOME

Sometimes the greatest support and kindness you can give another is providing a temporary foundation for them to just be so that they can get their own footing back.

I lived in the San Francisco Bay area among the dot.com entrepreneurs. We gave all our time and energy to our jobs, our dreams, the million-dollar idea, to going public and cashing in. Those stories do happen, and I'm glad they do because it keeps us motivated to create amazing concepts in our ever-changing world.

But in that time and area, when you met someone new, you didn't ask "What do you do or where do you work?"

You asked, "Who are you with?"

That meant what start up, what dot.com, what idea, what venture capital company? A lot of my identity was wrapped around that world.

I was also far enough into my marriage where we decided to try and get pregnant and start a family. We were going to start a new phase of life and identity. But life wasn't all perfect! There were obviously challenges in the marriage that are easier to see now years later.

Over the course of three months, I found myself fully struggling with my marriage, laid off without a job, and newly pregnant. Life had put not one but three bumps right in my path. Yes, I was grateful I was pregnant, but it certainly wasn't an idyllic life set up.

I felt alone.

I felt shattered.

I felt crushed.

I felt betrayed.

I felt less than.

I felt lost.

Because I had some free time with no work, and things to work out in our marriage, we took a trip to the Bahamas. We went to Bimini, Bahamas, which was known as Ernest Hemingway's favorite escape with aqua blue waters and magical healing elements. We had been there before and were familiar with the island and even the island's dive operators. They had been on the island for over two decades and saw tourists come and go. On a previous trip, I had connected to the wife in charge of the business. She had a huge heart and an even greater sense of people and intuition.

I remember just going through the motions of the trip. It's true that wherever you go, there you are. I was on a gorgeous island, but all the issues I had to deal with were there. I honestly don't remember a lot of that trip until the end. It was the day to go home, whatever that was at that moment, and I did *not* want to go home. I felt as if I didn't have a home to go to, a job, a purpose, or anything. I was newly pregnant and felt guilt that I should be beyond elated, but instead I was lost. I decided to stay. *Alone.* The dive operator found a little apartment that I could stay in for a week before the next tenant was settling in.

But she went beyond that. She sensed how vulnerable I was feeling. How utterly lost. She opened her heart and her home to me. I remember her seeing the look on my face and she knew I didn't want to be *alone.*

We were looking at the closet to put my things and she held my shoulders and said, "You're coming home to my house."

Yes, I knew her from one or two previous dive trips and emails, but she fully opened her home to me. She had children of her own, a business to run, husband, friends, life, and more. She even moved people around the house all so I could have a safe loving place to *just be.*

To sleep.

To feel loved.

To feel heart.

To feel acknowledged.

To feel whole.

To celebrate new life and my pregnancy.

To rest.

Plus, social connection.

I learned true kindness.

Opening one's home when someone is in need can build a foundation inside a person way beyond the four walls, food, and time that you give. I fully remember walking into her daughter's room and feeling welcome. I remember the pillow, the fan to keep cool, and drawer she cleaned out for me to put my things. I really didn't want her to go out of her way anymore than she already was, but it was just her loving way.

I believe the universe, or the spirit or God puts people in our path when we need them most. I saw love, joy, laughter, the lighter side of life, a slower pace, healthy marriage, motherhood, and other ways to live life than I had been living. I had not been around children much, and I got to spend time with her three-year-old and eight-year-old daughters and their playful spirits. It was a glimpse of life ahead for me.

Sometimes we need to ask for help. And that's ok. The best thing we can do as kind humans is to let people know that each person is a precious soul. I only stayed a week, but I was taught a lifetime of lessons.

You see, when someone has temporarily lost their footing in life, then it leaves feelings of uncertainty and worry. We know we're the only ones who can free ourselves from the sinking feeling and it's a daunting task. If you can help provide moments of reprieve from that feeling of losing her or his established foundation, it gives someone the boost of feelings to move forward. It's hard for many of us to ask, but admitting you need help is a powerful thing. It's humbling and creates openness between people. Most people like to help each other, and you create new bonds that go beyond the situation. It did exactly that. It's almost two decades later and we are still close friends. She is still kind as ever. I watch her grown daughters do the same kind things that she does.

The beauty of their kindness was how they let me experience life in their world. The time with them wasn't discussing my problems late into the night and hours of talking. Their kindness was shown in such a deeper and open way. They let me experience life. Just to *be*.

I remember the simple details of walking places to run errands, taking a moment to snap a photo of her daughter being silly on the corner of a building, making cupcakes, sipping iced tea, learning a listening-skill exercise from a recent Tony Robbins retreat, sweeping away sand from the day, riding in a golf cart with their dog leaning against me, and Oreos at sunset.

After a week, I felt stronger. Loved. Cared for. Carefree. Generally, their kindness reminded me that everything would be okay. The kindness of opening their home to me gave me hope and my footing: priceless gifts.

LEANN SPOFFORD is an experienced marketing advisor, author, nature enthusiast, and epigenetics lifestyle coach at the Apeiron Center for Human Potential. She is the founder of Creative Content Connects, which helps businesses remember their whys and creatively communicates that why so they connect with their customers and others.

Leann is known for her unique branding process: Remember Who You Are. She created Nature's Beauty Project to raise the conscious awareness of our planet and the inspiration from nature's beauty. Leann is currently writing Nature's Beauty Inspires.

Connect with Leann
Website: creativecontentconnects.com
Website: epigeneticsretreats.com
Facebook: NaturesBeautyProject
LinkedIn: leann-spofford

CLOSING

We want to thank you for joining us on our mission to spread more love and kindness in this world. We hope you have found this book so inspiring that you will continue in your new role as a Kindness Crusader. It doesn't take a lot to be kind, acknowledge someone, stand up for someone, or just show someone that you care.

The best part of being a Kindness Crusader is it feels just as good, if not better, to be the giver. Your vibration will rise in joy and happiness, which in turn will raise the vibration of those around you. We do hope that you will continue to give the gift of kindness and plant those seeds everywhere you go. Thank you for being a Kindness Crusader and thank you for helping us to make the world a better place. From our heart to yours, many blessings to you.

Love,

Kim Richardson

Kim Richardson
Publishing

CALL TO AUTHORS

Do you have a book inside of you that is ready for the world to see? Have you ever thought about sharing your story?

Everyone has a story and I believe that by sharing our stories, we may be of service to someone else that has had a similar experience. We all learn and grow from each other. You and your lessons are a valuable asset to this world! Nothing brings me more joy than assisting others in bringing their dreams to reality and helping others to live their best life.

Everyone has their own reason for becoming a published author. Whether you are looking to create a book to support and market your business, looking to leave your mark behind in this world, or just a burning desire to help others, I would love to assist you in your journey to becoming a published author.

It is my desire to be a part of raising the vibration of the world, helping everyone to see the love within themselves and each other. Will you join me?

Perhaps you have a book already published or ready to market. I offer many services such as; book cover design, 3D book images, marketing images for email and social media, marketing videos, all to highlight your beautiful project. Perhaps you have always dreamed of having your own card deck, I'd love to help your dreams become a reality.to learn more about the work I do, visit; KimRichardson.Kim and check out my online courses here; kimrichardson.kim/online-courses.

If you would like to get notified of up and coming publishing opportunities, sign up to get notified here; kimrichardson.kim/call-to-authors-1

I look forward to working with you! Peace, love and light,
Kim

KIM RICHARDSON is a personal chef, mind, body, spirit practitioner, bestselling author and publisher teaching others how to live in a high vibrational place of peace, love, and joy. Through sharing her own personal experiences, she empowers individuals to transform their lives. She helps individuals to heal, forgive, and expand without judgment.

Kim teaches with unconditional love as she hopes it will have a ripple effect in the world. Her services include; health and spiritual coaching, small business consulting, book publishing, personal chef and catering, as well as transformational workshops and retreats. Be sure to visit her website to claim your free gift.

Author of the best-selling book, *High Vibe Eating, a Cookbook for your Mind, Body, and Spirit*
Publisher and co-author of the *52 Weeks of Gratitude Journal* and *Kindness Crusader*
Coauthor of *Living Your Purpose*, *365 Days of Angel Prayers*, and *Spiritual Leaders Top Picks*

Connect with Kim
Website: KimRichardson.Kim
Facebook: kimrichardson444
Email: Kim.Richardson@KimRichardson.Kim

Kindness Calendars & Bingo Cards

Visit KindnessCrusader.com to download and print your calendars and Bingo Cards.

There are also blank templates so you can create your own. Have fun with it!

January

Say something nice to each person who you come across	Help a mother struggling with her baby carriage	Put money in an expired parking meter	Don't interrupt someone when they are talking	Bring coffee to your spouse without being asked	Be appreciative & gracious when complimented	Drop off a meal to someone who is ill or elderly
Call the 1st person that comes to your mind	Put your hand on your heart and compliment yourself	Tell a stranger you appreciate them	Treat yourself to at least one hour of nothingness	Listen to your favorite music from high school	Make a meal for someone you know is hurting	Text someone you haven't seen in a long time and tell them you miss them
Cook yourself a hearty meal	Compliment three strangers today	Praise a coworker for their hard work this week	Let someone in line ahead of you at the store	Donate some change that's filling up your wallet	At some point today, show yourself self-care	Send love and healing to Mother Earth
Be kind to Mother Earth and animals- eat vegan today	Go for a walk and pick up trash	Spend time at an animal shelter loving on one of the animals	Send love and healing to Mother Earth	Gift a reusable bag to someone	Return a stray shopping cart, other than your own	Pay for the person behind you (coffee, tollbooth)

February

Daily dose of self-kindness with self-forgiveness	I am kind to my body today by accepting it exactly as it is right now	Daily dose of self-kindness with a hug to yourself	I am kind to my body today by moving it (exercise)	Daily dose of self-kindness with self-patience	Daily dose of self-kindness with a compliment to yourself	
Treat your co-worker to lunch for no particular reason	Say thank you to everyone who provides you a service	Offer encouragement to a child trying something new	Give a compliment to someone having a difficult day	Volunteer for a favorite charity or cause	Say good morning and good-bye to your co-workers today	
Let someone cut in front of you in line	Warmly smile at everyone you see today	Truly forgive someone today	Pack a care package for a deployed soldier	Spend some time with an older relative or friend	Find a way to be kind to yourself today	
Buy an item on a wish list for an animal shelter	Shovel snow or mow the lawn for anyone in need of assistance	Tell someone they are appreciated and loved	Offer a hug to anyone in need	Hug a tree, thank it and ground yourself	Smile as you hold the door open or meet someone	
I am kind to my body today by eating well						
Call a friend instead of text, just to say hello						
Buy a coffee for the person behind you in line						
Volunteer with a child to read to pets at a shelter						

March

Kindness CRUSADER

- Write an appreciative letter when signing a bill
- Allow another driver to take your great parking spot
- Take someone's grocery cart for them in the parking lot
- Give a generous tip for a job well done
- Place money in a diaper box at a local store for a new parent
- Offer to let someone go before you in the checkout line
- Compliment someone's smile or attitude
- Touch a life- take a flower to a shut in
- Touch a heart- send a card to someone you love
- Touch a life - compliment a coworker
- Touch a heart- hug a widow
- Spread Kindness- sincerely smile at those you meet
- Be a Kindness Crusader in all your actions
- Be kind to yourself- get enough sleep tonight
- Remember everyone is doing the best they can
- Offer a loving smile while looking in the mirror
- Nourish your body with a healthy meal today
- Thank your imperfections for what they teach you
- Give yourself permission to spend a day relaxing
- Give gratitude for your body
- Take a walk or exercise
- Write a kind post-it note and leave it for someone to find
- Make a thank you card for a community helper
- Listen attentively to someone and state back what you heard
- Volunteer doing something you are good at
- Encourage someone to not give up
- Tell someone to never forget how beautiful they are
- Give yourself permission to make a choice based on what you want

April

Make a meal for someone who is ill or need of support	Pay for the person behind you at a coffee shop	Help a person with their groceries in a parking lot	Mow the neighbor's lawn, or shovel snow in winter	Call someone who may be lonely or isolated	Check on your elderly neighbors	Let someone go in front of you in line
Leave positive affirmations in public places	Write yourself a love note	Practice deep listening today	Hand out a snack to anyone that looks hungry	Forgive someone you hold a grievance with	Make eye contact and smile at a stranger	Give yourself a huge hug and then kiss your hand
Run errands for a busy friend or family member	Lift someone up in prayer	Encourage someone that may be struggling	Be patient when someone is new at their job	Thank a military person for their service	Bring your neighbor's paper to their door	Smile at everyone you pass
Write a love note to a loved one	Say I love you from the heart	Lift up others by pointing out their goodness	Take action contrary to what you feel when it helps others	Only speak in kindness; Is it true? Is it necessary?	Send flowers for no particular reason	Take time to be grateful to your creator and count your blessings

May

Play an Eye-Spy Kindness game with yourself or a friend	Offer a compliment as a way of lifting others up	Leave some coins on a public bench	Write an uplifting message for someone to find	Commit to mirror kindness when looking in mirrors	Look for and acknowledge the kindness in your world	Offer a smile to those you feel need one
Buy a coffee for a stranger	Release a judgement you have about yourself	Look into the eyes of someone who serves you and smile	Look into the mirror and say something you admire about YOU	Write a love note to yourself	Write a love note to someone you love	Send a note to someone you admire and tell them why
Reach out to a family member you haven't spoken to in awhile	Smile and say, "Hi" to 5 strangers	Bring a plate of cookies to a neighbor	Send a thinking of you text to 5 friends	Look at yourself in the mirror and say I love you	Volunteer to help someone	Look someone in the eyes and let them know you see them
Be kind to animals, visit a shelter	Be kind to birds, put out birdseed	Be kind to the earth, pick up trash on a walk	Express appreciation to those who love and support you	Buy an extra lunch for a homeless person	Invite a new acquaintance to have coffee or tea	Show patience, tolerance and compassion to others

June

Buy your husband his favorite snack	Pick up that piece of trash that you see	Plan a surprise party for someone	Buy your spouse flowers just because	Refrain from posting negativity online, spread some kindness	Participate in a fundraiser instead of immediately saying no	Pick up that piece of trash that you see, and throw it out
Help someone before they ask	Pick up litter at the park	Compliment a stranger	Deliver treats to your local police station	Send a "thinking of you" text, to random contacts	Donate used books to the library	Let someone merge in front of you in traffic
Spend time playing a board game with a child	Offer someone who is having a hard day a hug	Ly your hand over your heart and say, "I am loved"	Post a kind note on a public mirror, "You're Awesome!"	Deliver cut flowers from your yard to a neighbor	Ask an elder person about their life	Write a card to someone who has touched your heart
Contact a woman's shelter to see what they need and make a delivery	Make sure your neighbor has their emergence preparedness kit ready	Gather friends to form a Kindness Crusader group	Secret Santa all year round	Carry Ziplocs of dog food in your car, for homeless dogs	Paint small rocks with inspirational words and leave them for others	Deliver a bag of groceries to someone in need

July

KINDNESS CRUSADER

Text someone you love a feel-good song	Make your favorite dessert and share it with a neighbor	Tell someone 5 reasons why you are grateful for them	Schedule a playdate with a child in your life	Cook a meal and share it with a busy family	Today give out 10 compliments event to strangers	Be as loving towards yourself as you are to others
Hold the door for 3 people	Offer to help someone doing chores	Teach someone something new	Be open to new ideas	Call your parents and tell them you love them	Cook for someone	Clean up garbage you see in the street
Write a positive review for a local business	Ask for a manager & compliment one of the employees	Give your UPS or FEDEX driver a bottle of cold water	Prepay the euthanasia fee at a veterinary clinic	Stick a kind note on someone's windshield	Put $5 for treats in your Red Box movie return	Tape spare change to a vending machine
Thank you for not littering	Laugh with a friend or a stranger	Wave at people as you go by	Listen without judgement	Give someone a hug	Be kind to the bees, the trees with thank you	Show love and gratitude to all

August

Kindness Crusader

Tell someone they are important in your life	Assume the best in someone else	Look for the good in others	Take your neighbor's trash can to the curb if they forget	Cook a meal for someone	Send a hand written note or card to someone
Be of service to someone you do not know	Be a billboard. Wear affirmative kind words	Always compliment a child's light up shoes	Say hello to someone new today	Declare today as Free Hug Day	Give compliments to every child
Donate your clothes you no longer wear	Do a chore you know nobody wants to do	Stop someone from spreading gossip	Drop quarters on the sidewalk for people to find	Smile at everyone you see	Leave a really good tip
Put a dollar in the pocket when donating clothes	Purchase an item you need from a charity	Host a party and have guest bring socks for a shelter	Be kind and patient to a person who is grumpy	Give a flower randomly	Forgive someone who hurt you
					Smile without expecting a friendly response in return
					Call someone you love
					Assist all with action

September

Kindness Crusader

Meditate for 10 minutes	Listen to Yoga Nidra on YouTube	List three things you are grateful for	Go to a park and bird watch	Kiss your partner for a few extra seconds	Decrease plastic usage, buy a reusable straw	Replace negative self-talk with positive ones
Help someone struggling with their packages	Treat others the way you would like to be treated	When you have a lot of something, be kind and share it	Seniors in your neighborhood could always use your help	Be open to receiving kindness, and you will get it in return	Truth and LOVE is always a kind positive energy	Honoring your oneness is being kind to EVERYONE
Listen to understand someone's fears	Clean a senior's house for them	Mentor a teenager	Empower a friend's lifelong dream	Be a reader at a library night	Teach how to play an instrument	Breathe with someone who is anxious
Offer to babysit for a friend	Cook a loved one's favorite meal	Write spontaneous kind notes to loved ones	Read to kids	Listen with your heart not with your head	Mentor and share your knowledge with someone	Encourage someone who may need it

October

kindness CRUSADER

RECEIVE - It allows another opportunity to GIVE	Spread kindness by doing something that brings you joy	Pay it forward - Repeat kindness you have received	A smile goes a long way & has a huge impact	Be contagious with your JOY!	Hold the door for someone	Show GRATITUDE w/a handshake & eye contact
Help a friend day! Offer to watch a friend's kids	Volunteer with your children day! Soup kitchen, etc.	Visit the elderly day - Read to them, make them cards, etc.	Write a letter to a soldier day	Donate clothes and toys	Deliver homemade goodies to first responders	Read your child a book about kindness
Pay for someone else's coffee	Meditate about loving kindness	Do a loved one's chore	Offer to shop for a friend	Self-care day, do something fun	Smile at a stranger	Send a thank you note to someone
Extend kindness to your closest loved one	Run through a sprinkler with young children	Visit a senior center and listen to one person's story	Bring a flower to a friend	Hold the hand of someone who is very ill	Read a story to a child	Pay for something for the person behind you

November

Kindness Crusader

Honor your body, compliment yourself	Open your heart to the possibility of kindness today	Give your time to a cause you believe in	Share a kind word with a stranger	Surprise someone and pay it forward	Eat yummy foods that are kind to your body	Take a moment and give thanks for a loved one
Take your neighbor a small gift just because	Take carnations to residents at a nursing home	Volunteer an hour of your time to someone	Take cards to patients at a hospital	Take your spouse to lunch	Send a thank you note to a school teacher	Thank and acknowledge a public servant
Be kind to yourself	Buy a coffee or tea for a stranger	Feed birds in the park	Give a hug to a stranger and let them know you care about them	Bring in baked goods for co-workers	Make homemade cards and hand out, just because	Pay for someone's parking
Buy lunch for the homeless	Visit a senior for lunch	Be the reason someone smiles today	Make a phone call to just say hello	Support to an artist	Thank the person directing you safely through road construction	Tell someone an inspiring story

December

Kindness Crusader

Invite a lonely friend to watch a comedy with you	Send an encouraging card to five friends	Send a real card to your own child	Take time to write & journal – know that you are important
Walk the dog for a sick neighbor	Leave an anonymous gift for your neighbor	Take your significant other on a surprise date	Strike up a conversation with someone standing alone
Include a lonely person in an outdoor activity	Get a massage and enjoy it with a friend	Have a family help a neighbor day	Forgive someone - Repeat as necessary
Dance with an elderly person to help them feel young again	Give a single parent "me" time	Encourage children	Create a magical fairy day for a child
Work on a special project that means something to you	Write positive reviews	Tell at least one person how great they are	Give yourself some recognition
Smiles are always free Smile!	Send a care package with a note to a soldier	Place encouraging notes under your families' pillows	Include someone new to your event
Donate supplies to homeless shelter	Sit with an animal at a shelter	Put on some music and dance, just for you	Place hot/cold drinks out for sanitation workers

B	I	N	G	O
Say something nice to each person you come across	Put money in an expired meter	Don't interrupt someone when they are talking	Drop off a meal to someone who is elderly or ill	Be appreciative and gracious when complimented
Help a mother struggling with her stroller	Bring coffee/tea to your spouse without being asked	Put your hand on your heart and compliment yourself	Tell a stranger you appreciate them	Cook yourself a hearty meal
Let someone ahead of you in line	Donate some change that has been filling your wallet	Kindness CRUSADER	Compliment 3 strangers today	Praise a coworker for a job well done
Gift a reusable bag to someone	Pay for the person behind you in line	Send a whimsical card for no reason	Give a random stranger a flower	Model kindness for a child
Be consciously patient with someone today	Smile and hold the door open for someone	Treat someone to lunch for no reason	Say thank you to everyone who provides you a service	Go for a walk and pick up trash

BINGO

Call the first person that comes to mind	Listen to your favorite music from high school	Make a meal for someone you know is hurting	Send love to Mother Earth and animals- eat vegan today	Spend some time at an animal shelter loving on one of the animals
Let the cook know how wonderful the food is	Return a shopping cart other than your own	Send an inspirational quote to a friend- anonymously	Smile at the stranger next to you in line	Greet your neighbor as you walk by
Volunteer for a favorite cause or charity	Visit a housebound senior who may be lonely	*Kindness CRUSADER*	Offer encouragement to a child learning something new	Tell a colleague how much any why you appreciate them
Leave a note in your child's, spouse's or roommate's lunchbox	Welcome a new neighbor with a sweet treat	Give a compliment to someone having a difficult day	Say good morning and good-bye to your coworkers	Let someone you care about know how important they are
Acknowledge when someone does something thoughtful	Leave a dollar for someone to find	Call a friend instead of texting	Be kind to yourself by eating well	Truly forgive someone today

B	I	N	G	O
Be kind to your body by moving it – walk, bike, take the stairs	Say "I Love you" to someone special, just because	Give a compliment to a stranger in line	Notice the kind people around you	Send a funny greeting card to a friend
Pack a care package for a deployed solder	Spend time with an older relative or friend	Warmly smile at everyone you see today	Volunteer with a child to read to pets at the shelter	Shovel snow or mow the lawn for someone needing assistance
Tell someone they are appreciated and loved	Offer a hug to someone in need	Kindness CRUSADER	Allow another driver to have your great parking spot	Be kind to your body by accepting is exactly as it is right now
Place money in a diaper box at a local store	Compliment someone's smile or attitude	Write an appreciative not when signing your credit card bill	Drop off unexpected cookies to your neighbor	Remember, everyone is doing the best they can
Be kind to yourself- get enough sleep tonight	Write a kind post-it note and leave it for someone to find	Make a thank you card for a community helper	Listen attentively to someone and state back to them what you heard	Treat yourself to one hour of nothingness

BINGO

Practice self-kindness with self-patience	Compliment someone you don't know for something positive you notice	Smile as you hold the door for someone	Buy an item on a wish list for an animal shelter	Buy a coffee for the person behind you
Give a generous tip for a job well done	Volunteer doing something you are good at	Encourage someone not to give up	Tell someone to never forget how beautiful they are	Lean in and ask someone to share their story
Let someone know they matter and share 3-5 reasons why	Leave positive affirmations in public places	Kindness CRUSADER	Run errands for a busy friend or family member	Be patient when someone is new at their job
Thank a military person for their service	Lift someone up in prayer	Send flowers for no reason	Play a game of Kindness Eye-Spy with yourself or a friend	Be kind to birds- put out bird seed
Share your lunch or snack	Invite a new acquaintance to have coffee/tea	Buy an extra lunch and give it to a homeless person	Instead of posting negativity online, spread some kindness	Participate in a fundraiser instead of immediately saying no

BINGO

Release a judgement you have about yourself	Help someone before they ask	Deliver treats to your local police/fire station	Donate used books to the library	Let someone merge in front of you in traffic
Spend a little time playing a board game with a child	Post a note on a public mirror that says, "You are Awesome"	Ask an elder person about their life	Contact a shelter to see what they need and do a delivery	Gather friends to form a Kindness Crusader group
Deliver a bag of groceries to someone in need	Paint rocks with inspirational words and drop them around town	*Kindness* CRUSADER	Carry a Ziplock of dog food in your car for an encounter with a homeless dog	Leave someone am anonymous surprise gift
Text someone you love a feel-good song	Make your favorite dessert and share it with a neighbor	Schedule a play date with a child in your life	Offer to help someone doing chores	Teach someone something new
Be open to new ideas	Call your parents and tell them you love them	Thank your imperfections for what they teach you	Cook a meal for a busy family	Write a positive review for a local business

B	I	N	G	O
Give your delivery person a cold water	Pre-pay for euthanasia fee at a veterinary clinic	Tape spare change to a vending machine	Put $5 in a Redbox movie return	Do not litter and pick up garbage as you walk by
Bee kind, the trees will thank you	Wave at people as you go bye	Express love and gratitude for all	Laugh with a stranger or a friend	Be kind to yourself with an overdue compliment
Assume the best in someone	Take your neighbor's trash to the curb if they forget	Kindness CRUSADER	Declare today as free hug day	Compliment the store clerk
Be of service to someone you do not know	Donate your clothes you no longer wear	Ask for a manager and compliment one of the employees	Be a billboard, wear affirmative kind words	Stop someone from spreading gossip
Spend time with your parents	Leave quarters for someone to find	Always compliment a kid's light up shoes	Share with a friend why they are a blessing	Look for the good in others

B	I	N	G	O
On a hot day, fill a cooler with waters to give	Put a dollar in the packet when donating clothes	Hold the door open for everyone today	Leave a positive review for a business	Give a flower randomly
Purchase an item you need from a charity	Be kind and patient to a person being grumpy	Forgive someone that hurt you	Mediate for 10 mins	Empower a friend's lifelong dream
Be a reader at the library	Mentor a teenager	*Kindness CRUSADER*	Offer to babysit for a friend	Go to the park and watch the birds
Buy a reusable straw to reduce plastics	Listen and understand someone's fears	Cook a loved one's favorite meal	Listen with your heart and not your head	Mentor and share your knowledge with someone
RECEIVE. It allows another the opportunity to GIVE	Listen to Yoga Nidra on You Tube	Accept others & their journey without judgement	Be contagious with your JOY	Show gratitude with a handshake or hug

BINGO

Volunteer with your children day! Soup kitchen, etc	Deliver goodies to first responders	Read to your child a book about kindness	Pay for someone else coffee	Do a loved one's chore
Offer to shop for a friend	Self-Care Day! Do something fun!	Send a thank you note	Help someone struggling with their packages	When you have an abundance of something, share it
Seniors in your neighborhood could always use your help	Run through a sprinkler with a child	*Kindness CRUSADER*	Visit a senior center and listen to one person's story	Hold the hand of someone very ill
Eat yummy foods that are kind to your body	Surprise someone, pay it forward	Share a kind word with a stranger	Open your heart to the possibility of kindness today	Thank and acknowledge a public servant
Send a thank you note to a teacher	Give a stranger a compliment	Take your spouse to lunch	Call a relative you haven't spoken to in a long time	Take cards to patients at the hospital

BINGO

B	I	N	G	O
Bring someone a small gift just because	Pay for someone's parking	Make homemade cards to give away	Bring in baked goods for other co-workers	Give a hug to a stranger and say I care
Buy lunch for the homeless	Pick up trash in your community	Give a stranger a compliment	Buy a teacher a gift	Smiles are always free! Smile!
Pay for the car behind in a drive through	Call a friend just to say hello	*Kindness CRUSADER*	Mow (or shovel snow) someone's lawn	Water someone's flowers or plants
Offer to watch someone's child	Be the reason someone smiles today	Tell someone an inspiring story	Thank the person directing you safely through traffic	Show support to an artist
Visit a senior for lunch	Put on some music and dance, just for you	Forgive yourself so that you can forgive others	Leave a kind comment on a friend's Facebook page	Show appreciate to another for just being them

BINGO

Invite an elderly person for dinner	Walk the dog of a sick neighbor	Give a flower to your mother and her old friend	Include a lonely person in an outdoor activity	Work on a special project that means something to you
Ask a person to carry their groceries	Encourage a child	Sit with an animal at a shelter	Send a care package with a note to a soldier	Give a single parent some "me" time
Write a positive reviews	Host a birthday party for a lonely elder	Kindness CRUSADER	Give yourself recognition and be proud of you	Leave an anonymous gift for your neighbor
Add encouraging notes to your child's lunches	Tell at least one person how great they are	Have a help a neighbor day	Forgive someone. Repeat as necessary	Include someone new to your event
Smile at everyone today	Send a real card to your own child	Send encouraging cards to five friends	Place love notes under your families' pillows	Strike up a conversation with someone standing alone